# Sew Wonderful Silk

*the guide to gourmet sewing
with silk & silk-like fabrics*

*by*
**Cheryl Arrants**

**with Jan Asbjornsen**

ILLUSTRATED BY DENNIS ARRANTS

EDITED BY KRISTI ST. AMANT

Cover Design by Cheryl & Dennis Arrants

Fashions Illustrated by Dennis Arrants,
with special thanks to Dover Publications,
New York, for supplying additional art.
ISBN 0-943704-02-2

SEW WONDERFUL SILK is dedicated to the
homesewer who is ready to step-up-to-quality.
We hope you enjoy reading and using the guide.


THANKS!

Grandpa and Grandma Sundberg. You made this
possible.

Madelyn Graham, Cheryl's first and favorite teacher
and couturiere.

Patrick Gallagher, always supportive.


A big thanks, too, goes to the companies we mention
throughout this book. Their products are pure
gourmet delights.


We name products we have used and enjoy. There
are many fine firms that offer quality items; we
could not possibly know or name them all. We offer
the names of those we trust as a basis for your own
comparison.

*Gourmet Sewing? Me?* YES!

Fine sewing is like fine cooking. Good results
come from quality ingredients, blended to perfection.
Just as a great cook won't settle for scrambled eggs
when the same ingredients can be savored as an
omelet, why should you make "another-O.K.-blouse",
when a sensational one can be made with the same
time and effort?

"I can sew a straight line," one of our students
told us, " but better fabrics intimidate me. If
someone would just hold-my-hand through the
process I'm ready to step up to quality sewing.
I'd love to make a blouse or dress that looks
custom-made instead of home-sewn." Now she does.
And, she spends less time and money doing so.
You can, too.

*Gourmet Sewing is an aquired taste.* Once you
try our suggestions, every garment you make
will be a pleasure to plan, sew and wear. Give
yourself this treat. Read through the book,
learn the art of gourmet sewing, and repeat this
phrase ," I will stay humble no matter how terrific
a seamstress I become." (It's going to be hard!)

*Cheryl*

# "Why Should I Sew With Silk?"

Any fiber that has been treasured for more than
than 5,000 years must be something special.
What is it about silk that inspires designers
to favor its use, and people like us to
find it sew wonderful? There are many reasons.
Here are four.

1. Silk is _practical_. A natural protein fiber,
silk breathes, making the fabric suitable for
year-round wear. Silk is strong; one filament
of raw silk has the same strength as a steel
filament of the same size. For years it was the
major fiber in parachutes!

2. Silk is a fabric of _value_. Good silk, given
the proper care, appreciates in worth through
the years.

3. The _look, feel and drape of silk is unmatched._
Drape any quality silk over your shoulders. Feel
its gentle warmth and smoothness, notice how the
sheen flatters your skin, watch your posture
improve to a slightly regal stance. This "Queen of
Fibers" performs subtle magic. You look and feel
better every time you wear a silk garment.

4. Silk is _sew wonderful!_ Follow our suggestions
and you will find silk an easy and joyful fabric
to sew  and care for. And, because you sew, your
choice of quality silks is vast. Ready-to-wear
can't begin to offer the selection and value in
affordable luxury that your fabric store can.

# "What About Synthetics?"

We love them! The techniques we use in this
book, along with much discussion, apply to
these miracle fabrics, as well as their sister,
silk.

# CONTENTS

## STEP UP TO QUALITY

## START FROM SCRATCH

## SELECT YOUR INGREDIENTS

# PREPARE

# BLEND

# SEW A SENSATIONAL BLOUSE

# EXTRAS

# SPECIAL TOPPINGS

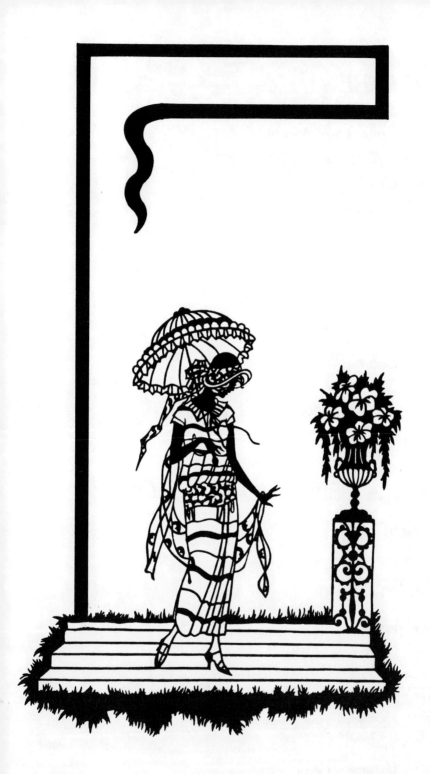

# STEP UP TO QUALITY

## Change Your Approach to Sewing

Do you usually: see a pattern you like, find a fabric that looks nice, take them home, quickly cut and mark, and <u>then</u> concentrate on sewing the garment? Most people do. We want you to change. Spend more time choosing styles and material, cutting and marking, and less time stitching clothes together.

Using this approach will save you time, money and frustration. No matter how skilled you are, a poor pattern choice, inappropriate fabric and/or sloppy preparation will result in clothing that is less than wonderful. Clothes you won't wear.

## Learn Quality in Fabric

Sensational clothing is always made from superb fabric. Learning to spot quality silks and synthetics takes time, patience and practice. Speed the process up by taking a crash course from the experts- designers.

a. Pad and pencil in hand, find a store that sells designer clothes. Seek out blouses and dresses.

b. Examine the texture, feel and drape of the fabrics used. This is known as *the hand of the fabric,* and tells you much about its worth. Designers use only the best material in the finest creations; the more you feel these fabrics the more familiar you will become with *the hand of quality.* (And your hand will remember!)

c. Read the labels, and note which fabrics you are drawn toward. What about the drape? Do you like crisply tailored pieces, or softly fluid lines?

Learn to *feel for quality* and you're half-way to successful gourmet sewing.

9

# Gourmet Fabric Stores

Search for your fabric store the same way you would seek out a fine restaurant or specialty shop. You want a place that shares your enthusiasm for quality material. Ask the following questions:

* Does the store offer a good selection of fine fabrics?

* Do the salespeople sew with these fabrics, giving them insight as to how they perform?

* Do you feel free to ask for personal attention?

* Is the store atmosphere a relaxed one? This is important. If you feel rushed you tend to make buying mistakes.

* Does the store have a full-length mirror near good lighting? You should always see the fabric up close to your skin, and learn its draping qualities. (More about drape on page 31 ).

Most good fabric stores, or departments, enjoy being *partners in gourmet sewing*. When you find such a store make use of its special services. Become aquainted with knowledgeable personnel. They sew, enjoy what they do and love helping you select clothes-to-be.

# Fabric Label

When you find a fabric that
matches the hand of one you
found on your *learning quality
from designers* trip note who
offers it (Brand), and/or the
origin (Country), what it's
made of (Fabric Content), and
what type, or weave, it is.
(See Silk Types page 20 for
help.) You will now know some
important facts about this material.

For example: You find a fabric that looks and feels
exactly like the one in the Calvin Klein blouse at
the designers' store. You note that the fabric is
offered by Stylecrest (brand) and/or comes from
Italy (origin). It is silk (fabric content) and is
a crepe de chine (weave/type). You know:
1. Stylecrest gives you quality you enjoy.
2. Italy produces some fine silks.
3. You appreciate the hand of silk.
4. You like crepe de chines.

This may sound very simplistic but knowing
what the fabric label means gives you two big
advantages when shopping for quality.

1. You always know exactly what you are paying
for; this is rarely possible in ready-to-wear.

2. You can ask the fabric store for material you
want in language you both understand, instead of,
"a-kind-of-soft-drapey-smooth-sort-of-fabric-like-
I-saw-in-a-blouse-downtown."

# START FROM SCRATCH

## How Fabric is Made

Learning how a fabric came to be will help
you determine what it can become.

The base of fabric is its yarn. There are two
types: *filament & spun.*

*Filament* yarns are long, smooth, continuous
strands, like those unravelled from silk cocoons.
These fibers are twisted together to form yarns
that produce smooth strong fabrics. Chiffon
and satin are examples of filament-yarn-fabrics.

*Spun* yarns are shorter fibers literally spun
together to form long strands. Spun yarn
fabrics tend to have less sheen, and a more
"hairy" appearance than filament based material.

Spun yarns are made from different lengths,
or *staples*. The longer the staple, the smoother
and stronger the fabric. Most polyesters are made
from long staple yarns. Wool flannel is an example
of the shorter staple yarn.

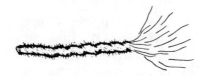

Yarns can be made into a variety of fabrics,
woven or knitted.

## Woven Fabric

Picture the pioneer woman, sitting at a large floor loom, interweaving her yarns, and you will have a good idea how fabric is woven. The only real difference today is that the looms are larger and automated. *But, some silks are still handwoven!*

The *warp* is the lengthwise, fixed yarn. The *weft* runs crosswise on the fabric, shuttled up and under, back and forth across the warp yarns. This is how a particular weave is made.

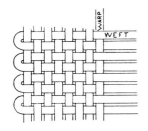

## Knitted Fabric

These are made by interlocking yarns in loops, much the same way people hand-knit sweaters. By looping the threads instead of weaving them the fabric will have more give, or stretch, to it.

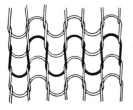

# Silk

Legend has it that a Chinese empress discovered
some worms spinning cocoons on the stems of
damaged Mulberry bushes, some 5,000 years ago:
She gathered several in her hands and dropped
them into a basin of warm water. The cocoons
began to unravel in long continuous strands of
exquisite threads which the empress had woven into
cloth for a gown.

For 3,000 years China held the secret of this royal
fabric. But, as with all great fashion ideas, news
eventually leaked out and Japan learned to produce
this wonderful fabric. Many other countries have
tried to produce silk, but today few do. Most of this
precious material comes from Japan, China, Italy,
France, Thailand and India.

## Cultivated Silk

Sericulture is the term applied to the art and science
of producing silk. It is an art because much of the
work is still done by skilled people. It is a science
because many conditions of growth are strict and
precisely carried out.

The silk worm is actually
a larva, most often of the
Bombyx Mori variety, that
feeds on Mulberry leaves. These worms
will eat for a solid month, shedding their
skin four times, and growing to a size
10,000 times their birth weight.

The larva will then spin a cocoon of protein filaments, *fibroin*, and excrete a glue-like substance, *sericin*, that will hold the protein in place.

The silk worm enters into a dormant stage, and begins to change into a moth. For breeding purposes, a few mothes will be allowed to hatch. Most, though, will have their cocoons slowly warmed, destroying the *chrysalis* inside while keeping the outside intact. The cocoons are then sorted according to size, color and general appearance.

These thimble-sized shells are bathed, to soften the gumlike sericin, and a reeler will pick up several strands, unwinding a group of cocoons together. Strands measure about 800-1,000 yards long! As the sericin dries it will "glue" the reeled fibers together. *This is raw silk- reeled silk, woven into cloth, containing most of its original sericin.*

Reeled filaments are classified and given grades, just like fine jewels. The International Silk Association accords merit to eveness, cleaness, length and tenacity (recovery after stretching).

Reeled silk is made into yarn by "throwing", or twisting it. High twists create crepe yarns, low twists produce satins.

The silk is bathed once more, to remove as much sericin as possible. De-gummed silk is the most lustrous, and expensive. Then...off to the weavers.

## Uncultivated Silk

Uncultivated silk, also known as wild silk, comes from worms living in natural conditions, feeding on a variety of leaves. They produce a coarser, more uneven type of silk, generally less expensive than cultivated silk. But that does not mean they aren't beautiful--just different. Tussah, pongee and some noils are examples of wild silk. (We explain more about these Silk Types, page 20 ).

## Doupion

This is a French term, meaning "double cocoon." It refers to silk that comes partially from the uneven filaments of cocoons that have grown together. The strands resemble wild silk.

## Spun Silk

When strands of silk are broken during reeling, or are just of shorter length, they are spun together to create longer strands. Because of their uneven lengths, the resulting fibers will have a slightly fuzzy texture and a duller appearance than reeled silk. Still, this form of silk is quite lovely as you will see in silk velvets and broadcloth.

## Weighted Silk

Silks that have been placed in a solution of metallic salts to give the illusion of luster and drape are known as *weighted silks*. They are sometimes used in ready-to-wear clothes to make a garment appear to be more valuable than it is. The salts are gradually removed by cleaning, leaving a faded, flimsy product. This is another advantage you have as a person who sews; you never have to worry about buying a weighted silk that will be worthless in the end. Fabric stores must label weighted silks. Few sell them. You can see why.

# The Great Pretenders – Synthetics

## RAYON

Rayon was the first imitation silk, developed in the late 1800's. We love it. Rayon dyes beautifully, drapes well and, depending on the rayon, feels like cotton. Rayon is sew wonderful to work with, too.

Basically, rayon is made from cotton and/or wood waste (cellulose) chemically altered into fabric fibers. There are two types of rayon: *viscose* (vĭs′ kōs) and *cuprammonium* (kōō pră mŏń nĕē ŭm).

*Viscose* rayons are made from spun fibers. They feel like a drapey cotton. Cheryl loves this type.

*Cuprammonium* rayons are made from a slightly different chemical base. The fibers are more filament-like so the fabric is shinier and less casual than viscose. This is Jan's favorite.

Hoffman California Fabrics offers great examples of both kinds. We think their prints are smashing! Stylecrest Fabrics imports sophisticated viscose rayons from Europe. Roth Imports and RJR also give you good selections of this sort-of-natural, sort-of-synthetic fabric.


## POLYESTER, NYLON, QIANA

Any of these make great wardrobe additions when they are produced with quality in mind. Though we feel that nothing matches the hand of silk, top companies manufacture some miraculous imitations.


These *great pretenders* are presented by: South Sea Imports, Seta Soie, Kabat, Stylecrest, Pago, Rosewood, American Silk Mills, Logantex, Hi-Fashion, John Kaldor, Loomskill, Apsco, Schwarzchild, Skinner, Thompson of California and SO MANY MORE!

# Blends

The purpose of blending different fibers together is to create a fabric with the attributes of all the fibers in the finished material.

Blending is generally done in two ways:

1. Different fibers are blended into one yarn, and then woven or knitted into fabric.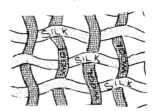

2. Different single-fiber yarns are woven or knitted together.

## Fiber Characteristics

Knowing the major characteristics of each fiber will help you understand how each benefits the other when blended. The following list briefly suggests how fibers complement one another.

Silk - adds luster, softness, drape, absorbency.

Rayon - adds drape, comfort, absorbency.

Cotton - adds washability, comfort, absorbency.

Wool - adds warmth, resiliency, comfort, body.

Linen - adds texture, absorbency, some luster.

Nylon & Polyester - adds strength, easy-care, and durability.

Percentage plays a part in blends. Adding a small amount of silk to a synthetic may enchance the fabric's prestige and price without adding to its overall quality. Ask store personnel to explain any blend you find confusing. You want to buy 100% quality...skip 5% prestige.

# Silk Types

This short glossary will give you brief descriptions of popular silks. Countries and/or companies that excel in certain types are mentioned to help you become more familiar with quality fabrics. Please remember that there are hundreds of fine firms. We could not possibly know or name them all. The few we note will give you a basis for comparison when you come across different brands.

These types are also available in silk-like fabrics. Please refer to *The Great Pretenders* for the names of some quality synthetic firms. They will be your guides.

*Take This Book To Your Fabric Store*

Seek out the types we list. It will help you to identify them easily. Then, the next time you see a beautiful dress in a magazine and you note the fabric is *silk crepe de chine* you will know exactly what that is, how it drapes and the average price per yard.

*Note*

We give you a few clothing suggestions in the glossary. For further help in selecting the right type for a garment see our *Fabric/Clothing Chart* on page__**32**___.

## Broadcloth (also called Fugi (foo' gee)

A lighter weight, plain woven fabric
made fron spun yarn. Tends to have less
sheen than other lightweights, but
still maintains silk's soft glow. Exotic
Silks, Schwarzchild Textiles and
American Silk Mills offer this fabric,
bested suited for crisper blouses,
dresses, skirts and men's shirts.

## Brocade (bro kad)

A midweight jacquard (see jacquard)
with a slightly raised design
on one side. Usually woven
with two or more colors, with
each side of the fabric appearing
different. China and Japan excel
here. Exotic Silks, Columbia
Fabrics and Stylecrest have
quality brocades which make
lovely kimonos, loungewear
and evening apparel.

## Charmeuse (shar moose)

A smooth and lustrous satin
with a soft crepe back. The drape
is heavenly. Horikoshi supplies
designers with this superb fabric.
Exotic Silks and Schwarzchild Textiles
both offer exciting colors in charmeuse.
(Keep in mind that the draping quality
of this silk varies depending on the
weight and thread-count- just like all
fabrics.) Although some people
feel this fabric should be reserved
for evening, we find this silk to be
versatile. From lingerie, to classic
blouses, to gorgeous gowns, charmeuse
is sew wonderful.

21

## Chiffon

The name comes from a French word
meaning "rag" or "sheer, flimsy cloth
that is strong." In silk it refers to the
very lightweight, sheer fabric that is
strong, with highly twisted yarns.
Chiffon dyes and prints well, and feels
like a feather next to the skin. Horikoshi
and Stylecrest present many colors
of this delight. Makes great overlays
for dresses, or can be used in several
layers by itself for flowing gowns.

## China Silk

This lightweight, plain woven silk is
made from silk "waste" (shorter silk
strands, end of the cocoon, slightly
uneven filaments). The silk has a crisp
rustling hand to it because it contains
quite a bit of sericin in it. China silk
does come mainly from China.

We reserve this silk for shaping
purposes only.

## Crepe (krāyp) & Crepe de Chine (krāyp dĕ shēen)

Crepe refers to either a highly twisted yarn
or a crepe weave. Crepe de chine refers to
lighter weight crepes. Both have a slightly
pebbly surface caused by the weave and/or
the twisted yarns. Both drape well. Crepe
is not as popular as Crepe de chine.
Crepe de chine is also a term that has been
used to describe any lightweight fabric. Once
you find "the real thing" you will never to
misled again.

Horikoshi supplies many top professionals.
Schwarzchild Textiles and Exotic Silks offer
crepe de chines in a variety of colors that
sew into beautiful dresses and blouses.
(See also Prints.)

## Faille (fāl or fīl) & Tissue Faille

Faille is a semi-lustrous, drapey silk,
woven with a crosswise rib. Tissue Faille
is a lighter weight version of this silk,
and is the more popular type.
Blouses, dresses, soft pants, evening
attire can all be made from faille
and tissue faille.

## Foulard (fō lärd)

This is a dress weight twill weave,
used in men's ties for many years.
Usually presented with small prints
or paisleys.

## Georgette

A lightweight sheer crepe, looser
and drapier weave than chiffon.
Silk georgette tends to "grow"
or stretch-out with wear, so
we reserve this fabric for loose,
special occasion garments.
Synthetic georgettes are among
our favorite silk-like materials.

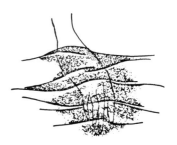

## Habutai (hắ bōo tā́ or hắ bōo tī́)

Japan originated this soft, downy,
plain woven silk. It is often mistaken
for China Silk, but Habutai usually
has a more opaque, even threaded
surface. Habutai is made from raw,
not waste, silk, so it can be made into
light garments as well as being used
as a shaping fabric.

Exotic Silks and Hoffman California
Fabrics offer habutai.

## Jacquard (jăk´ ärd or jĕ kärd´)

This is not really a type of fabric; it is a special weave that produces a figured pattern on cloth. Brocade is a type of jacquard. Damask is another jacquard; it looks the same on both sides of the fabric. The Orient has long excelled in silk jacquards which are imported by Schwarzchild & Exotic Silks. The French create silk jacquards from such fine filaments that the feel and drape of the silk is unmatched. Stylecrest presents these. Garments made from jacquards must be matched to the weight and drape of each fabric.

## Silk Linen

This plain woven silk is so much easier to sew and care for than flax linen. It tailors well and can be worn year round; great for travelling. Schwarzchild and Exotic Silks carry this gem all year.

## Noil (sounds like oil with an "N")

The word is French for "small knots in the cloth." Noil and Raw silk are often confused with one another. Noil is made from short and long filaments, yielding a silk with nubs, small knots, in the fabric. It varies in weight and quality. Great for casual outfits.

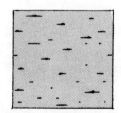

## Paillettes (pī yĕts or pā yĕts)

This term has two meanings:
1. A round sequin with one
hole near the edge.
2. A silk, usually chiffon, that
incorporates metallic chips
in the fabric's production.
This involves great skill
and time. The silk must be
of high quality, woven,
printed, screened with
adhesive, screened with the chips.
The results are exquisite and expensive.
The French are known for paillettes
and Stylecrest imports them with care.
Items requiring little yardage, like
caplets, scarves, overlays, etc.
make the best use of this sensational silk.
(Paillettes are always drycleaned by a
specialist. Ask the firm if they know how
to clean the silk.)


## Pongee, Honan, Shantung

All of these silks resemble one another. They
all tend to be hand-woven, slubby silk broadcloth
of varying weights. Although each has a definite
characteristic, they are so often misnamed that
we won't try to confuse
the issue. Just keep in
mind that which ever name
it is called, the fabric is
a high-sericin silk which,
depending on the weight,
makes beautifully tailored
garments. Exxlon and Exotic Silks offer these in natural
tones. Rodolph creates their own in Thailand, presenting
gorgeous screen printed pongees made from a blend of
Thai and Japanese silks. Classic and durable.

### Raw Silk

This refers to cultivated silk that has
been reeled, woven and still contains
most of its sericin.
Raw silk comes in
a variety of weights,
from sheer gauze to
heavy upholstery.
Most often offered in
its natural off-white
color, with tiny nubs.
Often mistaken for Noil.

### Satin

This is a lustrous silk made
from low-twist yarns. The warp,
or lengthwise yarns, float on
the surface to create a sheen.
Satin is not as drapey as
Charmeuse. Satin is backed
with a tightly woven side,
rather than a creped one.
Wellman and Exotic Silks are
just two of the companies that
offer beautiful satins in prints.
Many firms offer the traditional
bridal satins.

### Taffeta (tăf´ ĕ tă)

A crisp, plain woven fabric
that is smooth on both sides.
Rustles when handled.
Moire (mwă˝ rā or moré ā) taffeta
has a watermarked pattern on it.
This silk lends itself to evening
and bridal faire.

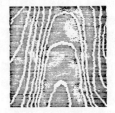

## Tussah (tŭ′ sǎ)

This is a wild silk that comes
from a worm releasing brown
or yellow toned filaments. Used
alone, Tussah yields a silk with
long slubs of natural tones, from
light to dark brown in color.
Combined with other silks, it
adds an interesting texture to
the fabric. Exotic Silks, Schwarzchild
and Stylecrest offer tussah that makes
easy-going dresses and sportswear.

## Silk Knits

Silk can be knitted like any other fiber. Jerseys
and boucles are popular silk knits. Fashion trends
seem to dictate the availability of these knits.

seem to dictate the availability of silk knits more
than other silk types.

## Silk Prints

You will find silk prints on every type we have
listed, but the most common silks printed are
crepe de chine, satin, chiffon, pongee and foulard.
Can prints be washed? Of course! The colors
won't run? Not if you purchase quality prints.
S. Rimmon&Co., Stylecrest, Rodolph, Schwarzchild
Textiles, Skinner,Wellman, Simone's Collection
are just a few of the many quality companies
that offer beautiful prints.

# SELECT YOUR INGREDIENTS

## Pattern Selection

Silk can be made into almost any article of clothing, from lingerie to sport clothes to eveningwear; it's such as versatile fabric!

For your first silk projects we have a few suggestions:

1. Make something with simple design lines. Show off that glorious fabric.

2. Make a comfortable garment. No matter how beautiful the silk, you won't wear the item if the sleeves are too tight, or the neckline feels to high.

3. Using a pattern you have made before is always a wise choice.

4. Our personal suggestion to students has been a sensational silk blouse. Basic but beautiful blouses never go out of style, are easy to make, require a small amount of fabric and provide the basis for a versatile and timeless wardrobe. On page **89** we show you a sensational silk blouse, and give you the step-by-step instructions to assure your successful completion of a silk garment.

# Fabric Choice

In no other area of sewing have we seen less
care taken than how a fabric will hang after it is
sewn. Great designers always drape ideas, and
so should you.

To emphasize the importance of fabric draping
we made two dresses, using the same pattern
and two different fabrics (both suggested by the
pattern.) Worn by the same person, one dress
appeared fun, kicky and fuller than the second one.
The other dress was breathtaking! The fabric
showed off the pattern's bias cut so beautifully.
At one of our fashion shows several guests asked
to see the garments up close, to assure themselves
that they were really made from the same pattern!
The characteristic drape of each fabric played a
critical part in the final appearance of the dress and
the wearer.

*Quick Drape Tips*

1. Pattern companies suggest two or more fabrics
on the pattern's envelope. Start with those.

2. Pick a few different fabrics and take them
to the store's full-length mirror (ALL fabric
stores should have one).

3. Unroll a few yards and drape as the pattern
shows. Gathered skirt? Gather up your fabric.
Using a border print? Drape it that way. Clingy
bias cut? Drape on the bias. These few minutes
will save you endless amounts of time, money
and the feeling that, "nothing ever turns out
like the picture."

4. REWIND the bolts of fabric.

5. Be a snob. Some stores (not the gourmet kind)
don't see the need for draping and frown on you
doing this. Turn your nose up and point it in the
direction of a store that appreciates your efforts
to create sensational results with their fabrics.

# Fabric/Clothing Chart

| TYPES OF SILK | EASE OF SEWING FROM 1-3 |
|---|---|
| BROADCLOTH | 1 (Very Easy) |
| BROCADE | 1 |
| CHARMEUSE | 2 (Easy) |
| CHIFFON | 3 (Not as Easy as 1&2) |
| CREPE | 1 |
| CREPE DE CHINE | 1 |
| FAILLE | 1 |
| TISSUE FAILLE | 1 |
| FOULARD | 2 |
| GEORGETTE | 3 |
| JACQUARDS KNITS | Depends on the hand. |
| LINEN | 1 |
| NOIL | 1 |
| PAILLETTES | 3 |
| PONGEE, HONAN, SHANTUNG | 1 |
| RAW SILK | 1 |
| SATIN | 2 |
| TAFFETA | 2 |
| TUSSAH & WILD SILK | 1 |

| BLOUSE | DRESS | SOFT SKIRT | TAILORED SKIRT | SOFT PANTS | TAILORED PANTS | JACKETS | LOOSER CLOTHES | EVENINGWEAR |
|---|---|---|---|---|---|---|---|---|
| GARMENTS BEST SUITED TO FABRIC | | | | | | | | |
| X | X | X | X | | | | | |
| | | | | | | | | X |
| X | X | X | | X | | | X | X |
| X | X | X | | | | | X | X |
| | X | X | | X | | | | X |
| X | X | X | | | | | X | X |
| | X | X | | X | | | | X |
| X | X | X | | X | | | X | X |
| X | X | X | | | | | | |
| X | X | X | | | | | X | X |
| Depends on the hand of the fabric. | | | | | | | | |
| | X | | X | | X | X | | |
| | X | X | X | X | X | X | | |
| X | X | | | | | | X | X |
| | X | X | X | | X | X | | X |
| X | X | X | X | X | X | X | | |
| X | X | X | | X | | | | X |
| X | | X | | X | X | X | | |
| X | X | X | X | X | X | | | |

33

# Buying Advice

* Give yourself time. Don't shop when you are tired, hungry, and the children are restless.

* Shop when the salespeople can offer you attention. This is very important if this is your first quality project. Ask for the advice of an experienced sales-person. If he or she is unavailable, shop when they are--make an appointment if necessary, but get that attention.

* Buy 1/8th yard more of any fabric if there is a question about care. You can use this extra amount as a test piece. Also inquire about excessive shrink-age. Even synthetics, like rayon crepes, sometimes shrink 1/3 yard or more!

* Buy your notions and shaping material now. It is hard to help someone select proper interfacing with just a verbal description of their fabric.

* S.A.V.E. (Stands for "Save Aggravation/Verify Endeavors") Record all purchases on quality fabrics. There are two good reasons for this.

1. If you fall in love with your new creation, a handy record helps you find similar fabric, style, or salesperson.

2. If something goes terribly wrong--the fabric changes color when labeled colorfast, for example, you will have easy access to the fabric store where the purchase was made and the clerk who helped you.

```
Date_____Pattern/Style_____
Fabric Brand/Origin_____
Fabric Content_____
Fabric Type_____
Care Label_____
Where Purchased_____
Sales Clerk's Name_____
Special Hints Given by Store_____
_____
Cost_____Swatch
Attach Receipt to back of card.
```

Keep a S.A.V.E. card in your purse and note your purchase at the time you buy the fabric. KEEP YOUR RECEIPT.

# Interfacing

One lovely quality of silk is the way it moves-
softly. Keep this in mind when choosing
your interfacing. It should
offer gentle support only.
When in doubt use the lighter
weight interfacing.

Select interfacing by placing
it under the silk and moving
the two fabrics together. This
will show you in an instant how
much body the shaping material
will add.

Don't be afraid to use more than one
interfacing in the same garment. A dress
with a crisp collar and soft front requires
a crisp and a soft shaping fabric.

The following list indicates the interfacings we prefer
when sewing with silk. Don't limit yourself to these.
New shaping material is added to the stores every
year. Experiment. We still do.

*China Silk & Habutai*
Cheryl's favorite for blouses and soft dresses.

*Polyester/Rayon Blend Interfacing*
Jan probably uses this type most often for her soft
or lightweight silks and synthetics.

*Woven Fabrics: Cotton, Batiste, Muslin*
Always a good choice for blouses and softly tailored
garments.

## Self-fabric Interfacing
You can use your fashion fabric as your interfacing if it is a lightweight material. We usually prefer to keep "the expensive stuff" where it will show--on the outside. If you do use self-fabric, cut the interfacing on the crosswise grain to provide more stability.

## Polyester Interfacing
Fine choice for synthetics and good on some silks, like softly tailored jackets.

## Acetate & Rayon Linings
Depending on their weight and crispness, these make great interfacings for collars, cuffs, shirt bands. Great with pongee and shantungs, too.

## Hair Canvas
This durable fabric uses a small amount of goat hair with wool, cotton, rayon and/or polyester. Used in tailored garments, canvas varies in weight as well as content. We prefer a wool, cotton, goat hair blend found in LADY HYMO. You can also use HYMO or ARMO P-1 for silk suitings.

## Sheer-weight Nonwoven Sew-in
Though we don't use any nonwoven fabrics in our silks or synthetics (they tend to inhibit the fluid quality of silk), we always keep some handy for reinforcing buttonholes. We'll show you how to use this later. Buy 1/4 yard of Pellon Sheer Weight Sew-in just to have on hand.

## Fusible Interfacing
Great improvements have been made in fusible interfacings the past few years. We love them for our synthetics. And a few raw silks and wild silks can fuse adequately. However, we generally don't use them on lightweight silks. You may want to try, though, so be sure to TEST IT ON A SCRAP FIRST! Fuse the silk, wash it, and then decide if bubbles or distortion will be a problem.

*SEE THE SHAPING CHART ON PAGE 38 FOR MORE HELP SELECTING INTERFACING.*

# Underlining

Underlining can add needed body where a more structured look is intended. Silk suitings that are a bit too fluid can benefit from this. Works wonders in the back of skirts and pants. When applied from the waist to the crotch it instantly gives a smooth  tailored fit, without the expense of lining the whole garment.

We underline with lightweight wovens (see interfacing.) Again, as you did when selecting interfacing, choose underlining by placing it with the fabric (and interfacing) to be used. Drape the material over your knee if that helps determine the final effect.
(See Shaping Chart page 38 for choices.)

# Lining

Lining can be a super finish on a garment as long as it doesn't inhibit the flow of your silk.

Our choices of lining include:

*China Silk, Habutai, Silk Broadcloth, Rayon, Acetate, Self-fabric, and fine pima cottons.*

*WE DO NOT USE SYNTHETICS TO LINE SILK.* Most synthetics don't "breathe", limiting the year-round comfort of your silk.

You can line synthetics with silk-like fabrics. Be careful, though. Lining a jacket with a lightweight polyester can cause problems. If you plan to wear the jacket over a silk-like blouse the two fabrics will slip and slide against each other until your jacket begins to fall back on your shoulders.  When this happens most people think the problem is with the fit not the fabric . Not true. Consider using rayon or acetate to line all suitings. They have a natural grab that will keep your jacket in place.

For more advise on selecting lining see our Shaping Chart on page 38 .

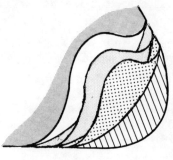

## Shaping Chart

| | BLOUSE & DRESS | TAILORED DRESS, SKIRT, PANTS | SOFT SKIRTS, PANTS | JACKETS | SHEER CLOTHES |
|---|---|---|---|---|---|
| CHINA, HABUTAI, SILK BROADCLOTH | I,U,L | U,L | U,L | UL | U,L |
| POLYESTER/RAYON | I | U,L | U,L | U | |
| COTTONS (BATISTE, MUSLIN, BROAD-CLOTH | I | I,U | | U | |
| SELF- FABRIC | I,U,L | | U,L | | |
| ACETATE OR RAYON LININGS | | I,L | | I | L |
| POLYESTER | I | I,L | | L | |
| HAIR CANVAS | | I | | I | |

Interfacing- I
Underlining- U
Lining- L

# Thread

Simply wearing clothes places the fabric under stress. The sewing rule has always been to use a thread that is weaker than your fabric. If too much strain is placed on, say, a sleeve, the thread will tear, not the fabric. Reweaving silk is not our idea of frustration-free sewing.

For the reason given above, some people will only use cotton thread when sewing silk. While this is a safe choice it need not be the only one. We use cotton, silk and long staple polyester threads to sew fine fabrics. All three have their advantages.

## Silk

Silk thread is spun silk, so it will match any natural fibers' qualities almost exactly. Jan loves the way the ultra smooth surface glides into her fabric, and sews with silk thread constantly. It is a very strong thread, though, and may not break under stress as easily as some sheer-weight fabrics. For this reason silk thread should be tested when you are sewing with chiffons, habutai or other very lightweight silks. Cheryl enjoys doing handwork with silk thread.
There are two disadvantages, or they appear to be disadvantages, concerning the use of silk thread:

1. Cost. Yes, silk thread is not an inexpensive notion. But, one spool of silk can add ease and quality to your sewing worth many times what you paid for the thread.

2. Colors. Corticelli Silk Thread is available in more than 35 colors. That may not seem like a wide color selection, but the silk used in thread starts out almost translucent. Even after dyeing, the thread will have a tendency to reflect the color of the fabric sewn. You don't need a perfect match when working with silk thread.

## Cotton

Cheryl uses this for most of her silk sewing. She likes cotton's stability and non-slick surface. Keep in mind that cotton does break under stress, and will eventually wear out. You may prefer a stronger thread when working with high-sericin silks, such as raw, noil, tussah and silk linen. Cotton is always a wise choice when sewing chiffon or other lightweight and/or sheer silks.

## Long Staple Polyester

This thread resembles silk thread in strength and smoothness. We use it on all synthetics, as well as silks that are not going to be tight-fitting garments. Silks with a high-sericin content sew well with long staple polyester thread.

Use a quality one- Molnlyke, Corticelli, or Metrosene are just a few fine threads.

## Extra Fine Cotton Covered Polyester Thread-CAUTION

J.&P. Coats produces Dual Duty Plus, an extra fine sewing thread, suitable for machine embroidery and some lightweight fabrics. This is an extremely strong and fine thread which withstands the stress of fast sewing during machine embroidery, and the particular fiber characteristics of certain synthetics, such as tricot and qiana knit. It's very nature of strength and elasticity gives Cheryl the thread she requires when working with those fabrics. (She wouldn't sew qiana without it.)
BUT, this super thread is not one to use on silk. It is simply too strong, too fine, and can cut the silk fibers. Use it as it was intended.

## Note

*We mix and match threads, too! We may sew the body with long staple polyester and topstitch with silk!*

# Tools

Just as a good cook enjoys working with the proper utensils, you will find gourmet sewing much more pleasant with the help of these supplies:

## *Extra Fine and/or Pleating Pins*

There are so many varieties of pins on the market that selecting suitable ones can be confusing. Standard silk pins are thick and rough tipped. These are intended for use with silks that have lots of the gumlike sericin in them--raw, noil, tussah. They are NOT the pin to use on lightweight silks. These pins can tear the fabric. *Pleating pins* are slim and sharp, and won't leave pin holes. We use this type of pin for practically all our sewing. Look for the word *pleating* on the box. (Or you can buy ones listed as "very fine silk pins".) WE DO NOT USE BALL POINT PINS ON SILK OR SILK-LIKE FABRICS (except knits). The tips are too rounded and leave pin-holes in the fabric.

## *Sizes 5-10 Sharp or Between Handsewing Needles*

Any brand will do. Betweens are shorter and stronger than Sharps. Cheryl prefers Betweens for hand-picking zippers and sewing hems. They keep her from taking too long of a stitch. Try a package of both. Keep in mind: the higher the number, the thinner the needle. Attach a button with a #5 or #6, him with a #8 or #10.

## *Beeswax*

Draw your handsewing thread through this and watch tangles disappear!

## Machine Needles

Use needles intended for woven fabrics. Size 10/11 (European 70) for lightweight fabric. Size 12/14 (80) for mid- to heavy-weight material. We have not found a #9 needle to be practical for most silk sewing. The thread does not glide through it easily.

## Shears & Scissors

Both should be in mint condition. Dull or nicked cutting tools will catch and pull threads on find fabrics. Gingher produces shears that are truly a sewing treasure.

## Muslin

We use a top-grade muslin to clean our shears and scissors, and for various other uses. Buy one yard and keep it handy. In future chapters we will explain its purpose.

## Vinyl Tablecloth, with Flannel Back

This will be helpful when cutting your silk or other slippery fabrics. More on page 54 .

## Rayon Seam Tape

Because Rayon has a natural fiber base, it tends to ease and press well. We prefer it to synthetic seam tape when used as a seam binding or stabilizer. Not all fabric stores stock rayon tape. ASK. Good substitutes can be made by cutting bias strips of rayon lining. (We explain the uses of this notion throughout the book.)

## Nylon Mesh Strips

These lightweight seam enclosures are nifty notions. They can be used in place of rayon seam tape.

## Scotch Magic Transparent Tape

3/4" wide tape is always on hand.

## Marking Tools

We use any kind, or method, that marks the fabric
without leaving permanent spots.  Cheryl always has
a dressmaker's pencil handy.  Jan loves the new
water-soluble pens.  Chalk is a good choice.  Just
don't use serrated tracing wheels to mark silk.  It
stresses the fabric.

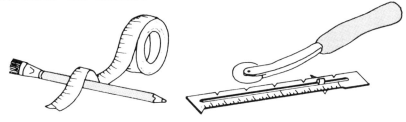

## ITEMS WE DO NOT RECOMMEND WHEN SEWING SILK

### Pinking Shears

Pinkers are an expensive investment.  While this tool
is a great asset to some areas of sewing, we don't
feel pinking shears are very useful in sewing silk
and silk-like fabrics.  The fabrics dull the blades
quickly, and pinkers require special care to keep
them in top form.  Reserve this purchase (or their
use) for tailored items of wool.

### Glues used for joining fabric and/or to prevent excess ravelling

Liquid adhesives have become popular
sewing notions, and for good reason.
When applied correctly, to appropriate
materials, they provide great results.
BUT, in order to be effective, glues
must be absorbed into the fabric. Natural
fibers, such as silk, are very absorbent.
The glue, whether white or clear, thick
or thin, may be absorbed into more than
just the area you wish to cover, leaving
you with a permanent disappointment.
For this reason, we do not recommend the
use of glues on lightweight natural fibers.

43

# PREPARE

## Prepare Your Machine

When was the last time your gave your machine a tune-up? A machine suffering from the "grundgies" skips stitches, makes funny knots on the bobbin side, and generally wreaks havoc on your nerves and your fabric.

Take out your instruction manual...the one that came with the machine...the booklet with all the dust on it...and do a thorough job, preferably the day *before* you plan to sew.

1. Use a small brush to remove line. Brush any area of the machine you can reach, inside and out.

2. Oil any metal parts that rub together.

3. Adjust the pressure regulator. "What?" Your pressor foot pressure regulator. The dial, button or screw that determines how much force is placed on any given fabric as it feeds through the machine. If you have never touched this item, it is probably set at medium. (That's why wool sews great and crepe de chine puckers like crazy!) Lighten the pressure. The manual will tell you how; what a difference it will make. *Some new machines have automatic regulators. Check your manual!*

4. You will probably need to lighten the thread tension, too. Your fabric is soft and relaxed so your machine should react in a relaxed manner also.

5. If you machine comes equipped with a throat plate that has a small hole, use it instead of the regular plate. It will keep silk from being drawn into the machine. <u>It is for straight stitching only</u>.

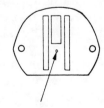

6. Find an empty bobbin. Don't wind thread on a bobbin that already contains thread. It can cause the bobbin to wind unevenly, feed unevenly and drive you crazy, wondering," What's wrong with this stupid machine?!"

Check the bobbin for small nicks, burrs, on the side. If you spot any throw the bobbin out. They cause thread to break.

7. Change the needle. No excuses. It is an inexpensive way to prevent skipped stitches, and unnecessary wear and tear on the machine.

8. Place a typewriting pad under a portable sewing machine to keep it from sliding on your table.

9. To keep slippery fabric from sliding off your table, pin or tape muslin or felt to your sewing table. This can be a real nerve saver!

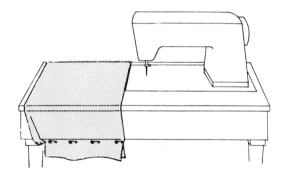

10. Stitch through a piece of muslin to absorb excess oil, and leave it under the presser foot overnight. Place another piece of muslin (about 14"X14") by your machine for later use.

11. *Definitely give yourself a pat on the back, and a light gourmet treat (something with a wine sauce). Afterall, you did open your sewing machine manual... finally.*

# Prepare Your Fabric

For years the process of preparing fabric for cutting has been called *preshrinking*. And, many fabrics did shrink. Some still do; rayon crepe is a good example.

Today, most fabrics are preshrunk at the mill. Does that mean your fabric is ready to cut? No. Your lovely piece of silk or synthetic has been wound on a bolt, wrapped and shipped across the country, or even around the world, to your store. This puts it under a mild stress which must be eased so the fabric will hang correctly in a garment. Think *pretreat*, not preshrink. And don't skip pretreatment or your clothes will suffer from puckered seams, uneven hems and the like. Enough said.

## Pretreating Synthetics & Blends

Follow the care instructions given on the bolt. Use detergent, too, to help remove any light finish applied to the fabric in order to make bolting easier.

PLEASE! Be cautious in your use of fabric softening dryer sheets. They can leave oily-looking spots and/or streaks on fine fabrics. The spots will look like fabric flaws, and are very hard to remove. The stuff coats the dryer so wash the inside out with soap and water to clean off any excess. Liquid softeners, used in your washing machine, are safe.

## Care Labels

One question we are constantly asked is, "Why does the bolt say 'hand wash, drip dry' and I know this fabric can be machine washed with no problems?" The answer is simple. People often abuse fabrics and then blame the manufacturer. To prevent possible complaints, the mill will usually put the most conservative label it feels is needed for a fabric's care.

This is yet another advantage to sewing; you can ask your fabric store how best to care for your purchases. If the answer is different from the care label, note it down along with the name of the salesperson on your S.A.V.E. card (page **34** ).

# Washing Silk

"You mean there are some silks that are washable?"
Yes! Even though most silks are labelled "dry clean"
you can safely wash them if they meet three requirements:

1. The silk must be colorfast.

2. It should not come from a country, or firm, that
practices old methods of dyeing or printing.

3. It must not change texture dramatically when exposed
to water.

### Determine Colorfastness

1. Heat iron to wool/steam.

2. Dampen a small piece of cotton or a cotton ball and
place it over a corner of your silk.

3. Cover the area with a dry press cloth and press for
about 10 seconds.

4. If no color or pattern appears on the cotton
your silk is colorfast.

There is an exception to the above. If your silk is
a dark or intense color, it may bleed, but not fade,
when wet. You may wish to wash 1/8yard of black,
fushia, etc. if you have doubts, and compare it to
the remaining piece. Bleed refers to excess dye; fade
refers to removal of dye.

### Countries that Practice Old Methods

Your store should know the origin of its silk. Read
the label and ask for care instructions. India, for
example still exports many silks that are handscreened
with natural dyes. Beautiful but not washable. Again,
you can test by washing 1/8 yd.

Silk is bathed in water several times during its production, so water does not damage silk. But, water
can affect dyes, prints, types of weaves, etc. Any
dramatic change in the *hand* of the silk is your sign
that the fabric would be better off dry cleaned.

1. Wash 1/8 yard of silk with lukewarm water and
mild soap.

2. Rinse with cool water and press between two
terry towels until silk is almost dry. Press with iron
set on wool/steam.

3. Is your test piece stiffer than your remaining
silk? Did it shrink alot? Does it look different--
less crepey, for example? Are the results in any way
negative?

4. There are no hard and fast rules concerning this.
Chiffon is normally dry cleaned because it will shrink
up after washing, requiring lots of pressing to
restore its original size. Jan doesn't mind the slight
surface change that occurs when she washes
Charmeuse. Cheryl always dry cleans hers. It can
be a matter of choice.

## Waterspots

While water does not hurt fabric, it can change it as
we noted above. That's what a waterspot is; nothing
more than a textural change that occurs when water
drops on any susceptible fabric. If the spot is
noticeable, because the fabric's texture changes in
that area, it is called a waterspot.

A waterspot is not a stain. Having the silk dry
cleaned will usually bring back a uniform texture to
the fabric. Even rubbing the silk against itself will
sometimes accomplish this. Just don't panic if your
silk waterspots; they will come out if the silk is a
quality one.

## Pretreating Washable Silk

Wash any silk that can be hand washed; even if you plan to dry clean the finished garment. By exposing it to water, you will prevent waterspotting later, make it possible to remove small stains between cleanings, and see for yourself what a strong, resilient fiber it really is.

Keep in mind that silk is an animal protein. Treat it with the same gentle respect you give your hair.

1. Fill a basin with warm water and a mild soap or detergent. Ivory Bar Soap, a PH balanced shampoo or any gentle solution is fine. DON'T use regular laundry detergent. You would not apply it to your hair; too harsh for you, too harsh for silk.

2. Place your silk in the water and swish it around for a minute or two. There is no need to soak it. DON'T rub it; you can hurt the weave or dye, not the silk

3. Rinse the silk in lukewarm/cool water. Squeeze, don't wring, out excess water.

4. Roll silk in terry towels to remove more water, and allow to dry as smooth and flat as possible (on a table or rack).

5. Press while the silk is still a little damp. (If the fabric dries completely, it may feel slightly crisp. Steam pressing will remove the crisp hand.

*Sometimes, when we are anxious to sew, we roll the silk in the towels several times, and then press on wool/steam until the silk is dry. Takes about 5 minutes from start to finish! Be sure to press the entire piece and then repress; don't press one small area until dry--you want it to dry evenly.*

## Pretreating Drycleanable Silk

You have a choice:

1.  Send the silk to the cleaners and ask them to "steam press" your fabric.

2.  Do it yourself. This will save you time and money, and you have a pressing board at your house anyway. *Your Bed!*

Your bed has built-in layers of padding which will absorb steam completely, while allowing your fabric to relax in one piece.

1.  Set your iron on wool/steam.

2.  Lay the fabric on your bed, folded or unfolded, right or wrong side up. It doesn't matter.

3.  Hold your iron 2" above the silk and allow the steam to flow into the fabric.

4.  After the entire piece is moist, allow the silk to set for about 20 minutes, or until completely dry.

5.  While the fabric's fibers are relaxed, relax your own "fibers" with a cup of tea.

*Note:*
*If you are concerned about a non-colorfast silk bleeding onto your bed, toss an old sheet on the bed first and steam the fabric right side up. We have never had any problem since we work with quality silks only.*

# Cut

Are you ready to slash right into that piece of stuff? Or, are you like most newcomers to silk--a little nervous? We hope you are just a bit anxious. It will make you cut your georgous fabric slowly and carefully.

## General Tips

1.  Press your paper pattern with a low-set dry iron.

2.  Lay fabric on a flat surface; even a clean linoleum floor is super.

3.  Use lots of pins. Since we use pleating pins, we never have to worry about pinholes.

4.  Pinning the selvages together can be a big help when working with lightweight fabrics.

5.  Check the grain. Fluid silks love to move.

6.  Cut, using long strokes, not short jagged ones.

7.  Cutting with the right or wrong sides together is a matter of choice.

### FABRIC WEIGHTS

Fabric weights are used by professionals to replace some, or all pinning. While they are helpful in providing extra stability on fabric, they are not a substitute for pinning lightweight silks.

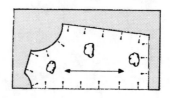

Weights are available free; you have them in your home. Small canned foods, bean bags, knoves and fabric-covered stones all make great weights.

Place weights on pattern grain lines, and pin fabric. Heavier fabric and skillful cutting requires weights only. Practice!

# A Common Pattern Alteration

The most common pattern change we have to make when sewing with silk is in the shoulder area. Silk drapes so well that even your always-fits-perfectly blouse pattern may appear to be slightly larger through the shoulders when made from charmeuse or crepe de chine. Then, again, it may not, so..... play it safe:

1. Raise the cutting line at the base of the armhole 3/8", tapering at the notch. Do this on the front and back. Note the *original* cutting line on your fabric, using a dressmaker's pencil or chalk.

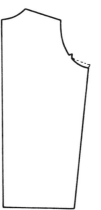

2. As you sew the garment, try it on before applying the sleeves (or baste in the sleeves if that helps) to see if shoulder width will be too wide.

3. If the shoulder is too wide cut 1/4-3/8" off the top of shoulder, starting at shoulder seam and tapering to notches on each side. (By adding 3/8" to the base of the armhole we created the correction for this alteration- your armhole is now the same size it would normally be.)

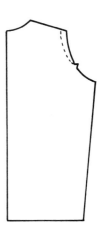

4. If the shoulder width is fine, trim off the extra 3/8" you added to the base of armhole and proceed.

# Cutting Different Silk Types

### Silks with High-Sericin Content

The gum-like sericin found in some silks (raw, noil, tussah) may cause the folded fabric to stick to itself in an uneven way. Place a piece of tissue paper between the two layers of silk to correct the problem.

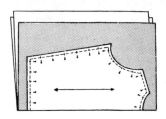

### Slithery, Slippery Silk

Charmeuse, satin, chiffon and other silks that are quite fluid may require a stabilizer. We use a flannel-backed vinyl tablecloth. It provides a *grab* for these extra-slippery fabrics, yet your cutting surface remains flat. And, you can cut on your dining table without fear of shear scratches.

When the silk is ultra slippery, turn the cloth to the flannel side and use that.

This handy accessory is worth its weight in gold if you are planning to do more than one silk project. But, if this is a one-time-only venture, or the stores are closed and you are ready to cut NOW- use an old sheet. Make certain it is not part of a matching set because the pins will tend to catch the sheet and you will probably cut into it more than once.

## Varigated, Patterned, Plaids, Super Slippery

You may want to cut this silk one layer at a time. For sections normally placed on the fold, such as backs, trace a duplicate piece on tissue paper. Tape it to the original pattern piece, and cut as one pattern section.

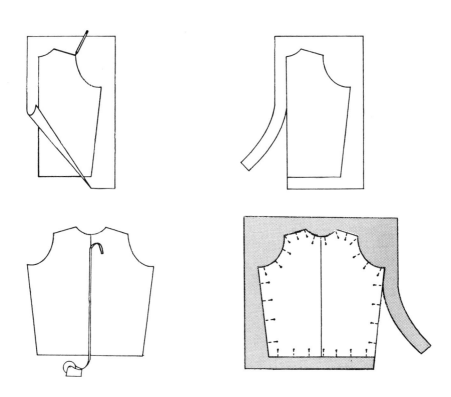

## Sheers

Whenever possible, eliminate facings and substitute French Piping instead (page 103 ). It will give a better look to the finished garment.

## Napped Silks

Satin, charmeuse and silk velvet have a definite direction or nap in the fabric, just like some prints. Hold your silk up one way and then turn it upside down. The fabric will appear lighter or darker, depending on how you hold it, if there is a nap. The most common solution is to lay all the pattern pieces in the same direction. You can also do what we have done on occasion...ignore the nap. Cut the fabric as you would normally, and allow the light to catch the sheen of your silk in different ways. What a glorious look! *We don't do this with velvet--too much contrast.*

## After Cutting Your Fabric

Your shears may feel slightly dull, due to a build-up of sericin on the blades. Cut into your muslin with several long strokes to clean them off. Great for removing synthetic fibers that also dull shears.

## One Last Suggestion

If this is your first silk project, and everyone is calling you today, the cat races across your table, and the whole baseball team wants cookies, STOP! This is no place to cut.

Ask your fabric store if there is a time you can use one of their cutting tables. Most stores can accommodate someone in the early morning or at dinner time. BRING YOUR OWN EQUIPMENT, and pick up after yourself. Don't be afraid to ask; special stores offer special services. This may be one of them.

# Bias Strips

You will find bias strips used throughout the book. Here are the basic instructions for cutting them.

1. Find the true bias by folding the crosswise grain to the lengthwise selvage. Press or mark along the fold.

2. Cut along the fold, then seam the cut end to the other end as shown. Mark the width of the strips desired.

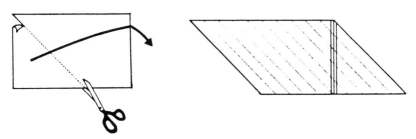

3. Right sides facing, match your lines. (This may seem awkward, and there will be an extra strip at each end. Stitch a 3/8" seam.
This is now a tube you can cut in one long strip.

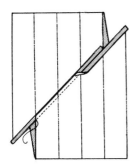
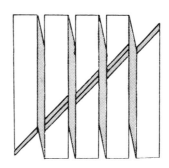

Though this is an easy technique, you may wish to practice on cotton, or other less slinky fabric, first.

# Mark

We make most of our silk garments from simple,
classic designs, so little marking is required.
Because of this we literally *snip* our way through
dots and notches, taking small 1/8" clips in the
seam allowance at these marking points.

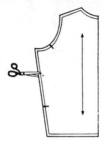

Where snips aren't possible (dart points, for example)
we use dressmakers' pencils or chalk, or water
soluble pens.  Test your tool on a fabric scrap to
determine the color and pressure needed for marking.

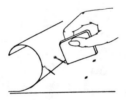

Using pins to mark can be helpful, if you are working
with a silk with a high-sericin content that holds the
pins in place, and if you use pleating pins to prevent
pinholes later.

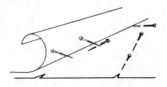

## Modified Tacks

Some silks require more secure marking. Light chiffons tend to lose pin-marks, and steam fades the pencil markings. You can Tailor Tack (SLOW) or use snips and *modified tacks* (FAST).

1. Snip any mark you can reach on seam allowance. Pin-mark any markings that can't be snipped: darts, casing lines, etc.

2. Using a single strand of a contrasting thread, draw the thread through each pin-mark twice. Leave long ends at beginning and end of stitch. Cut thread, and remove pin. The thread will stay secure until you are ready to remove it.

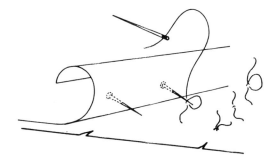

Notes

*Please test any marking method on a scrap first.

* You may want to mark the wrong sides of any fabric that has a close appearance on both sides.

* Marking is the last slow step in sewing your garment. Accurate marks insure quality results, so take your time.

# BLEND

Because cutting and marking can be time-consuming, you may think that sewing the fabric will be slow going, too. Not so! Silk is one of the easiest fabrics to stitch and press!

## Stitching Tips

1. Before you stitch on your silk, sew across your muslin to catch any excess oil left from your cleaning the machine.

2. Keep the stitch lengths in mind:

| | | |
|---|---|---|
| Sewing Regular Seams | lightweight silk<br>midweight | 12-15/inch<br>10 |
| Staystitch | lightweight<br>midweight | 10-12<br>same |
| Ease | light or mid | 8-10 |
| Gather | lightweight<br>midweight | 10-12<br>6- 8 |
| Reinforce | light or mid | 15-18 |
| Topstitch | lightweight<br>midweight | 9-12<br>6- 8 |

Do you know what your machine sews when set at different stitch lengths? Don't rely on what your manual tells you. Even the same model of the same brand can vary. Check you machine's settings by stitching on muslin with a dark color, using different stitch lengths. Count the exact number per inch and note the results in your manual. (One of our students found her machine stitching 9 per inch when the setting indicated 6; she had the machine adjusted and found topstitching easier after that.)

3. Keep the fabric taut,
not stretched, while
stitching.

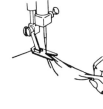

4. After a seam is made
*gently* remove the silk from
the machine. Yanking can
cause pulls and tears in
the material.

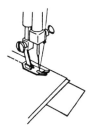

5. Stitch with the natural
grain of your fabric to
prevent stretching and/or
puckering.

6. Need extra stability when
sewing super slippery silk?
Place a sheet of typing or
tissue paper under the fabric.
(This will dull your needle
faster- keep this in mind.)

7. If you are sewing with silk thread and the spool is
unwinding too fast (because it's so slick) place your
spool in a mug or glass behind the machine and thread
normally. This creates a longer up-hill route for the
thread, slowing it down a bit.

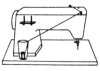

8. Any time the machine starts to make funny, clunking
noises while you are stitching, the cause is probably a
build-up of sericin on your needle. Stitch a few rows
on your muslin to clean the needle.

# Easing & Gathering

Learn the difference between easing and gathering and all your garments will have a more professional look.

## Easing

This is done whenever you want to gently reshape a section, such as a sleeve cap, to conform smoothly with an adjoining section, like the armhole.

A longer stitch length of 8-10 per inch allows the fabric to ruffle slightly. You can then coax it into place with your fingers, pins, or steaming.

Areas you may need to ease include: back shoulder seams, princess seams, sleeves, skirt waistlines applied to waistbands, hems.

## Gathering

This is done when you want to draw-up fabric tightly and evenly before joining it to another section, as you would a gathered sleeve cap.

Silk and silk-like lightweights require a stitch length of 10-12 per inch to gather. This shorter stitch length gives you good control over where, and how much, gathering is desired. Two rows of gathering stitches affords even greater control.

Midweight fabrics can be gathered using a longer stitch, 6-8 per inch.

Areas to gather include: sleeve caps and cuff-lines, waistlines, ruffles, some yokes.

### Note

We ease or gather using 1/2" as our seam line. If we stitch two rows of gathering we stitch 1/2" and 3/8" from edge of fabric.

# Taping

Certain sections of a garment may need to be stabilized to prevent the fabric from stretching out of shape; or eased into a more fitted shape. Taping provides fabric control without creating a stiff appearance.

You can tape with rayon or twill tape, as well as a strip of selvage from any lightweight fabric.

## Taping to Prevent Stretching

Simply stitch tape over a seamline, stitching along the 5/8" seam.

Prevents stretching or stress on: shoulder seams, fitted waistlines, gathered seams, yokes.

## Taping to Create a Fitted Shape

1. Using the pattern, not your fabric, as a guide, cut the tape the length of area to be shaped. Could be a roll-line, pocket slant, V neck.

2. Pin tape to top of placement line. Lay tape along line, and then pull it *past* the line's end about 3/8". Your fabric will buckle. Good.

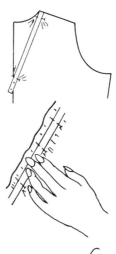

3. With your fingers, gently press the tape and fabric together so that buckling is evenly distributed along line. (Think of this as finger-easing.) Pin along line. Fabric should be flat where tape is pinned even though it will still buckle slightly on either side of it.

4. Stitch along both edges of tape, or down the center of it. Steam press lightly to help ease fabric and remove most buckling. The finished section will hug the body and never lose shape. BE CAREFUL NOT TO CUT THROUGH TAPE AS YOU CONTINUE TO SEW. IT WILL WEAKEN THE SHAPING.

# Mistakes

Everyone makes mistakes when sewing, even the best pros. We certainly do. Knowing when to rip out an error is one good sign of a real professional.

This can be an important lesson if you want to step up to quality sewing. Some fabrics can wear out from too much stitching-then-ripping--not to mention the sheer frustration caused by removing the stitches from a seam 6 times!

We have our own philosophy about mistakes. If the error doesn't affect the *fit, function or appearance* of the garment then leave it alone. But out comes the ripper if even one of these areas is affected.

## Example

You are making a lined blazer with welt pockets on the inside and outside. The inside pocket has crooked "lips." DON'T RIP.

* No one will see it, so it doesn't affect the appearance.

* The pocket is still functional.

* It certainly won't change the fit of the jacket.

But, say, the outside pocket also has welts that are uneven. RIP!

* It will affect the appearance of your garment. Make any adjustment needed to meet the three requirements.

*Many of our students keep this picture and the three requirements given above on their sewing room bulletin boards. It gently reminds them: fashion-not-frustration.*

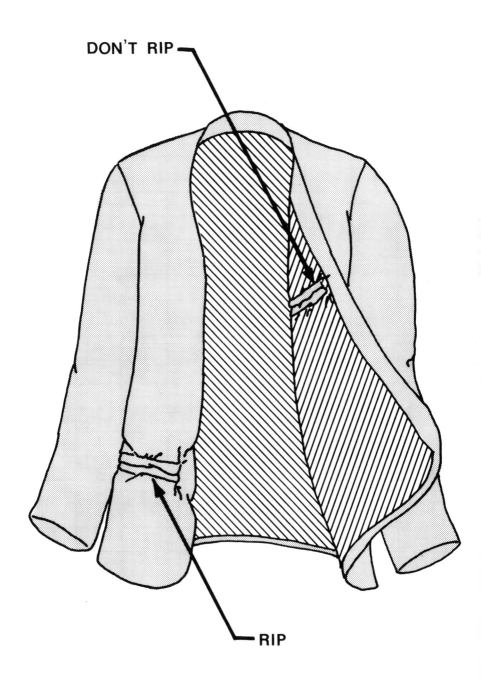

DON'T RIP

RIP

# Pressing

Too many people look at pressing as a minor part of sewing. But think for a moment. Before sewing machines were invented, garments were *persuaded* into shape by pressing tools of one kind or another. Hand stitching held a dress together; pressing formed the fine contours by stretching, shrinking, flattening, fluffing, hiding or highlighting certain features.

Today's sewing machines make garment construction so much easier that you may forget that 50% of sewing is *pressing*. Remember this and all your clothes will take on a custom-made appearance.

## Equipment

### Iron

Your iron is second from your machine in importance. You don't need a fancy one. A good steam iron will do fine. If you would like to invest in a top-notch iron that will give you years of service, we recommend three:

1. Proctor-Silex 1510L. This is Cheryl's all-time favorite. The burst-of-steam keeps working after constant use, and the plastic water reservoir prevents rust from forming in water.

2 & 3. Sears 6214 & Sunbeam 1291. Both are burst-of-steam. Their water reservoirs contain small jewels to prevent rust deposits in the water.

### Press Cloth

After all these years as sewing partners, we still prefer 100% cotton flour-sack towels, found in dime stores. They are large, last forever and provide good heat/steam control. Batiste makes a great shear press cloth which we use when we really need to see the fabric below. *We always keep one cloth reserved for fusible application. It is marked on one side with a scrap of fabric sewn to a corner. When fusing, this side is kept facing up to prevent a build-up of fusible debris on the iron.*

# Ironing Board Cover

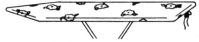

It may seem silly for us to care what cover you use on your board but let us explain. Many covers have silicone finishes on them to prevent scorching the fabric when using a high heat and/or starches. Also, the finish reflects heat which the maker feels will speed up ironing.

Today's fabrics don't require high heat or heavy starches, so the disadvantages of this cover begin to appear. The heavy finish doesn't allow steam to pass through the board quickly, slowing you down as you wait for the fabric to dry. Secondly, the finish can flake off onto fine fabrics, leaving you with gold or silver dots that, on silks or synthetics, are hard to remove. Speed-up pressing safely. Use a cotton cover. *June Tailor* offers a good one...or you can make your own! It's easy and fast.

## How To Make A Cotton Cover

a. You will need 1-3/4 yard 100% cotton, 35 - 45" wide--it can be a print, if of high quality; 4 yards single or double folded poly/cotton bias tape; 4 yards strong cord (or the old cord from your present board cover); thread. Use your present pad or buy cotton padding.

b. Use your present cover as your pattern. Flatten it out and cut out your fabric.

c. Cover all edges with bias type to form the cord casing. Leave a small opening at one end.

d. Tie a knot at one end of the cord and slip the other end through the casing using a bodkin, or tied to a safety pin.

Save the old cover for future replacements. Make two so you can wash one. Makes great gifts.

## Pressing Board

Custom houses use large pressing tables, not
skinny ironing boards, to press garments
during construction. The wide flat surface
provides for faster pressing because the
fabric can be moved to one side to dry
while another section is pressed, all without
stressing the garment.

Your dining table makes an excellent pressing
table, and so does the top of a wide chest of
drawers. Throw a sheet or vinyl tablecloth
over your pressing surface and you're half
way to custom house standards. All you
need now is a *pressing board*. This you can
make, in about 5 minutes!

Materials: FREE! An empty bolt from your fabric
store (most stores would love people to help
rid them of this excess cardboard.), two old
terry towels or scraps of 100% wool, enough
100% cotton to cover the bolt, plus 1/8 yard.
*We like to match our pressing and ironing
board covers, using the same cotton.*

1. Preshrink cotton 3 times.

2. Wrap padding material,
the wool or towels, around
bolt.
Secure with pins or tape, just
to keep it in place.

3. Wrap bolt with cotton like you
are wrapping a present, turning
under raw edges. Pull cotton snugly
into place and hand stitch in back.
You won't know how you got along
without this once you use it.

## Other Helpful Pressing Tools

There are many but we recommend three:

1. An iron cleaner, to keep your second piece
of sewing equipment in tip-top shape.
2. June Tailor's Tailoring Board and top
cover. This is a modified version of tools
used in custom houses. It is not a necessity,
but we couldn't sew without it- good tools for sewing
spoil you, like good kitchen utensils. This is
an expensive item so be convinced you understand
its use. Ask your store for a demonstration.

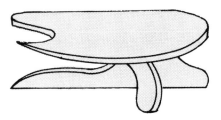

3. Home Tools- you have lots! Rolled up towels
are great sleeve boards, rolling pins are super
seam boards. You need not invest a fortune
to have a fortune's worth of tools.

## Pressing Tips

1. Always press a seam in the same direction as it was stitched. This will help the thread sink into the seam and ease out puckers.

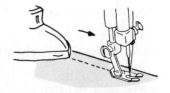

2. Pressing on the wrong side of the fabric prevents unnecessary stress on material. Using a press cloth on the right side also protects your silk. *But, don't work yourself into a frenzy if you forget either of these things– silk is very strong and resilient.* It is a dream to sew and press.

3. Allow fabric to cool after pressing, otherwise pieces can stretch and look worn-out before your garment is even finished. This is why a pressing table and board are so helpful. Gently moving a pressed piece to one side will still allow it to cool on a flat surface.

4. Use a good hanger, plastic or padded, to hold the bodice while you work on sleeves or collars, or other sections. Saves on wrinkles and more pressing.

5. If you press in a crease on a washable silk spritz a little water on the crease and repress it out. No water spot will form on pretreated washables.
If the item is only drycleanable and a waterspot forms, that's OK, too. Finish the garment and have it drycleaned to remove the spot.

# Seam Finishes

A proper seam finish will help assure a *long-life* garment. There are many appropriate seam finishes for silk and synthetics. We will show you our favorites.

## Double Stitched Seam

Use this on any lightweight fabric.

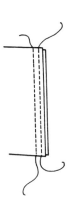

1. Stitch a normal 5/8" seam.
2. Stitch again, 1/4" from seam line.
3. Trim fabric close to stitching.

## Blindhem Seam Finish

Even most older machines have this stitch; a series of straight stitches with occasional zig-zags. It is best when applied to one seam allowance of midweight fabrics.

1. Stitch a normal seam. Press seam open.

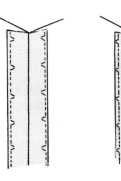

2. Stitch the blindhem; stitch along edge of seam allowance. You can sew the stitch with the zig-zag pointing in or out from seam edge depending on how you hold the fabric.

3. Trim close to stitching.

## French Seam

This truly professional finish is very easy and fast to sew. It also protects your fabric for longer wear. Apply to any straight seam of light-midlight fabrics.

1. Stitch a 3/8" seam, using 15 stitches per inch, wrong sides together. Trim to 1/8".

2. Press seam open with tip of iron.

3. Fold right sides together and press along edge. This will insure a smooth seam line. Pin lightly if necessary.

4. Stitch 1/4" seam, right sides together. This creates an enclosed seam.

5. Press sides and shoulder seams toward back, and sleeve seams toward front. This prevents bulk at seam joinings later.

Small french seams may ripple at the shoulder line on lightweight fabrics. This is due to the slight bias line of shoulder cuts. To prevent the ripple:

1. Follow step 1, except stitch a 1/4" seam. Don't trim.
2. Follow steps 2 & 3.
3. Follow step 4 except stitch a 3/8" seam.
The larger seam will lie better.

*To finish curved seams on garments using french seams see the next seam finish.*

## Modified French Seam

The following two methods can be used to enclose
seam edges on straight & curved seams.

*Method 1 (slow)*

1. Stitch a normal seam,
right sides together.

2. Fold in 1/4" on each seam
allowance, stretching curves
slightly to maintain smooth
edges.

3. Stitch edges together.

*Method 2 (Fast)*

1. Stitch a normal seam,
right sides together.

2. Trim seam to 1/4".

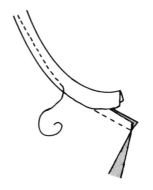

3. Fold and press a
strip of rayon tape,
or use Seams Great.

4. Enclose the raw
edges of the seam
allowances together.
Press lightly.

# Hong Kong Seam Finish

Named after the tailors who made it famous. This finish is great for unlined garments made of midweight fabrics.

1. Use rayon tape or bias strips of lining( see bias strips page **57** )1/2-3/4" wide. Do not use synthetic tape or lining. It just won't apply properly.

2. Stitch a normal seam. Press open.

3. Right sides together, stitch tape, or lining strips, to one seam allowance. Use 15-18 stitches per inch and a 1/8" seam allowance.

4. Fold tape over seam allowance and press.

5. Fold tape under edge of seam allowance and stitch next to, but not on, tape. This secures the tape to the underside of seam allowance. (If it turns out that your strips are too wide, simply trim them in back after stitching.)

6. Repeat the above for other seam allowance.

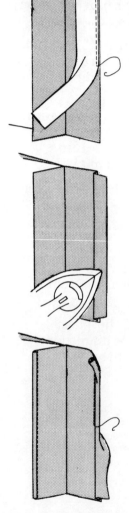

*Note*
*Finish curved seams using modified french seams, page* **73** .
*Be sure to remove an unlined jacket so everyone can "ooh and aah" the superb finish!*

# ZAP! Zig-zagging

WE DO NOT USE ZIG-ZAG STITCHING AS A
SEAM FINISH ON ANY LIGHTWEIGHT FABRIC.

* The back and forth movement of thread on finer
fabrics ripples the seam allowance, causing a puckered
seam line.

* The large amount of thread used for zig-zagging a
seam can add noticeable bulk to a lightweight fabric.

* Every time the garment is laundered the seams will
tend to pull-up, making pressing very tedious.
(All of us put off ironing garments that are a hassle,
and so the clothing doesn't get worn- not a good
investment.)

* There are other seam finishes that will create silk
sensations, inside and out. So Zap! the zig-zag.

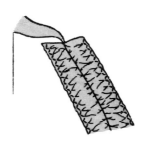

# Zippers

When sewing with silk suitings, such as tussah
or silk linen, a regular zipper will serve nicely.
Lightweight silks call for a softer touch. Several
companies produce feather-light coil zippers that
look like knitted mesh. Don't let looks deceive you.
These fasteners are very strong.

You can apply your zippers entirely by machine,
as you would normally, or, for a couture finish,
handpick the zipper in place. Not only will it
look better but the zipper will lie flat, and the
process only takes a few extra minutes.

## Handpicked Slot

1. Baste the zipper seam line closed,
and apply a seam finish.
Press open.

2. Open the coil zipper
and place it face-down
over the seam so that
the teeth of one side
rests along the seam.
Stitch one side of zipper
to one seam allowance, 1/4"
from the teeth.
The seam line provides a guide
so no pinning is needed. We
sew from bottom to top to
maintain the grain flow of
our fabric.

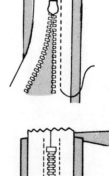

3. Close the zipper, and
stitch the remaining side
to the other seam allowance.

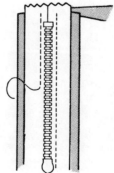

4. Turn fabric to right side. Lightly finger-press a strip of 3/4" wide Scotch Tape over the seam line so that 3/8" falls on either side. This will be your seam guide.

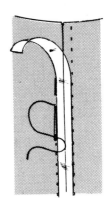

5. Draw a single strand of thread through your beeswax, and then secure it to the wrong side of fabric by taking several small stitches in one seam allowance.

6. Starting at the base of the zipper, bring thread up to right side next to tape. Stitch zipper and fabric together, using small evenly spaced pick-stitches.

*Pick-stitch:* This is made by bringing the needle to the right side of fabric, putting it back through the material and zipper *just behind the first spot where the thread came up,* and then moving it forward about 3/8". Repeat the picks, never pulling tightly.

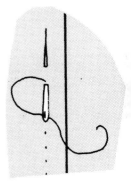

7. Secure the thread to the top of the zipper and cut. Starting at the bottom, repeat the process on the other side.

8. Remove basting and tape. Press lightly. Done correctly, the stitches will barely show. *We know several people who apply all their zippers this way. You can't see small mistakes and it goes in so easily!*

## Placket

1. See step one of first
zipper method.

2. Placed closed zipper
face down, with teeth <u>next</u>
to, but <u>not on seam.</u>
(We sew the zipper from bottom
to top, so zipper will lie to
the right of your seam line.)
Stitch, matching edge of
zipper to edge of seam allowance
only.

3. Turn zipper so it faces up.
This creates a small fold in
the seam allowance next to
the teeth. Stitch along this
fold from bottom to top.

4. Turn zipper face down
and match free edge to other
edge of seam allowance. (You
will notice a small pleat form
in seam. Good. Stitch zipper
to this seam allowance.

5. Press lightly and turn
to right side of garment.
Place a strip of 3/4" wide
Scotch tape lightly over
seam so that 1/2" falls to
the left of the seam. This
is your stitching guide. Handpick just the left side of zipper
in place as you hand-picked in
the first method.

6. Remove basting, tape, and
press lightly. Your machine
stitched side of zipper will not
show. Superb!

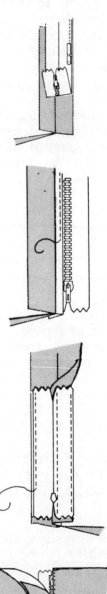

# Buttonholes

Whether you make machine or handsewn buttonholes they will go in easily if you slip a piece of Pellon Sheer-weight Sew-in interfacing just where the buttonholes will be made. It keeps the fabric stable, preventing the fabric from pulling or puckering. *Do this on lightweight fabrics even if you have already interfaced the buttonhole area.*

* Slip small pieces or a long strip of the Pellon between the facing and the garment.

* Make your buttonholes.

* Snip out excess Pellon until only the buttonhole area has the interfacing in it.

*Reinforced Buttonholes*

For a more professional looking buttonhole:

* Make the buttonhole as instructed above.

* Slash the hole open carefully.

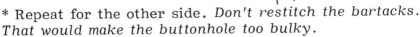

* Starting at the top of one side, restitch one side of buttonhole, using the same small zig-zag width. Hold the hole open with your fingers. The zig-zag overcasts the edge, so all loose threads are covered!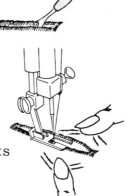

* Repeat for the other side. *Don't restitch the bartacks. That would make the buttonhole too bulky.*

* You may wish to try different sewing feet to achieve the best results; a satin stitch foot or your regular foot.

# Buttons

When you make silk clothing the fabric is the attention-grabber, not buttons. Select yours with care so the fabric and buttons don't compete. Keep them simple.

Mother-of-pearl, wood or other "naturals" make great silk additions. Covered button are always a good choice. We offer two methods of making them.

## Method 1    Fast & Easy

Maxant and other companies make a covered button kit that comes with its own applicator. They are great, but they have two problems you should deal with.
1. They come with metal caps which show through lightweight fabrics. Underline your button circles with a second, smaller circle of your fashion fabric or an underlining.

2. The smooth edged caps don't always grasp slippery material securely. Apply a dot or two of fabric glue just before you put the shank in place. The button will usually stay together.

## Method 2    Not Fast but Easy & Secure

Use this method when your silk is too slippery for Method 1. Charmeuse would fall into this category.

1. Buy a button kit that contains button caps with teeth. (The kind that tear off your fingernails, the kind you hate.) These are super if you follow instructions.

2. Cut your fabric circles, then run a basting stitch, by hand or machine, along the outside edge.

3. Cut an underlining, slightly smaller than your circle and place this piece in the center of your fabric.

4. Place the button cap
on top of the underlining/
fabric and draw up the
basting thread. It will
cause the fabric to
encircle the cap evenly
and easily.

5. Using a pin or
seam ripper, not your
fingernails, tuck in
fabric where necessary.
No need to glue. Attach
button shank. Cheryl
prefers this method
on small buttons. No
funny tucks, no loose
button caps.

*Plastic Buttons*

Follow this custom tip for blouses that will be
tucked into skirts and pants- never worn
outside. Leave off the last one or two regular
buttons and substitute clear plastic ones.
They are flat so they won't show through
slim skirts or fitted slacks.  They also save
on wear and tear of nice buttons.

# Hems

When you are ready to hem, pin the recommended hem in place and try the garment on. Does the fabric drape well? If the fabric is a midweight suiting it probably hangs correctly. You can go ahead and hem as usual.

But, if you have made a fluid dress the hem may drape a little too well, shifting and sliding into an unsightly finish. *Bias garments always do this. See page* **106** . You can't change the natural drape of your fabric so change the hem. We offer you several.

## Narrow Stitched

Great on any lightweight fabric.
Can also be used on some midweights like
raw silk.

1.Place a row of stitching 1/2-1" from bottom edge.

2. Fold edge of fabric to the stitching line and press.

3. Fold again, just far enough to turn the stitching to the wrong side. Stitch close to folded edge, by hand or machine.

*Hankerchief Hem*

Do the same as above, but add an additional row of machine stitching close to the bottom edge of hem.

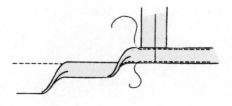

## Machine Rolled

Jan loves her hemmer foot, especially when sewing
sheer fabrics. Most machines, even old ones,
have a rolled hem foot, so check your manual.
You can also buy one to fit almost any machine.
Your machine's manual probably gives you some
instructions but we offer our own. Try this
on a scrap first. It may take a few minutes of practice
but you'll whiz through these tiny hems after that!

1. The foot looks like it has a
small funnel on it.

2. Fold your fabric twice (tiny
folds) and press lightly, for
about 2-3".

3. Set the fabric under your hemmer
foot and place the needle in the fabric.
Needle should be close to edge of fold.

4. Put foot down on fabric and stitch
for 2", using 12-14 stitches per inch.

5. Leave the needle in fabric
and raise the foot. Lift your
fabric until you can slip it into
the funnel part of your foot.
*Yes, it will seem confusing at
first.* Lower the foot again.

6. Holding the edge of your
fabric tautly with your right
hand, keep it slightly raised
and in line with the left edge
of the hemmer foot. Begin to
stitch, and you will see the
foot gently turning the fabric
and then stitching it in place,
in one step, creating a tiny hem.

*Don't give up if the first effort is less than perfect.
So was your first buttonhole. It is an accessory worth
using, so practice until you are comfortable with it.*

# Miracle Lockstitch

Cheryl loves handwork (Jan thinks she's crazy.)
This is her favorite hemming stitch. Not only is it
easy and practically invisible but it's also a great
one for people who step through their hems. You
can literally break half the stitches and still have
a sturdy hem! A Miracle!

We will show you how to apply this stitch on small
hems, but you can use it on deep ones as well.

1. Fold up a small hem twice.
Press.

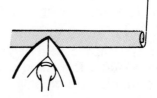

2. Draw a single strand of thread through beeswax.
(Out of beeswax? Draw the thread under a warm iron.
Yes! Press the thread for tangle-free stitching.)
Use a small hand needle, #8-10.

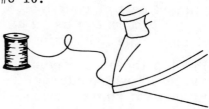

3. Secure thread with a few small·stitches in the fold.

4. Slip the needle into the fold and move 1/2" forward. Bring needle up through edge of fold.

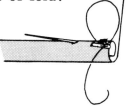

5. Circle the thread to your left. Catch one thread from the garment and one in the fold, next to your thread. Pull up the thread, locking the stitch.

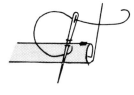 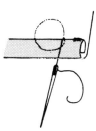

6. Take the next stitch by putting the needle back into the fold, close to the stitch you just made. Move it forward 1/2" and repeat the process around. End by securing the thread with small stitches.

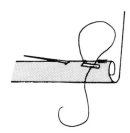

# Miracle Lockstitch Variation

## Hong Kong Hem

This is a great way to finish the hem of an unlined jacket that you have applied the Hong Kong Seam Finish to, or for deeper hems in suit weight fabrics.

1. Use the same material you used for your seam finish- rayon tape, China silk etc. See bias strips page **5 7** or Hong Kong Seam Finish, page **74** .

2. Apply the bias strips to the hem edge the same way you apply it to seams.

## Lace Hem

Another nice way to use the Miracle Lockstitch on deeper hems.

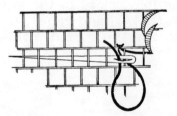

1. Apply lace to edge of hem by machine.

2. Secure your thread by making several small stitches.
Slip thread under the lace mesh for 1/2".

3. Bring needle up and circle it to the left.

4. Take one thread from garment and one mesh of lace and pull-up the needle as it goes through the circle. There is no need to pull the thread tight. A light touch will bring invisible results. Continue in this manner for the entire hem.

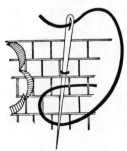

## Tailor's Hem

This is another way to hem suits or other deep-hem garments. The stitching is invisible, though not as secure as the miracle lockstitch. It does provide more "give" so that if your silk tends to shift, like faille for example, the hem will move with the fabric.

1. Pin hem in place and steam bottom edge only. (Never cover the entire hem with your iron-it will leave a hemline impression on the right side.)

2. If your hem needs to be eased into place, run an easing stitch 1/4" from top of hem, pull-up thread where needed and steam out fullness.

3. Finish top of hem with lace, seam tape, hong kong finish, or whatever you prefer. You may not even need a finish. Tissue Faille is better left unfinished, for example.

4. Secure thread in a seam allowance. Fold back hem 1/2" and pin. This will keep your fabric in place while you hem. Using loose stitches catch one thread of garment and one of hem, moving your needle forward 3/8" each time. Keep picking up one thread from garment and one from hem around the hem line. Secure thread, and press lightly.

*Note*
Deep hems may require two rounds of stitching, especially if your fabric is quite heavy. One row stitched 1 " from top another 1/2" from top will add support and prevent sagging in this situation. Coats usually require this method.

# SEW A SENSATIONAL BLOUSE

## Purchases

1. Choose a pattern that resembles the one shown here. Pattern pieces should include: fronts, back, sleeve, cuff, collar.
2. Crepe de chine- we recommend this type of silk for your first project.
3. Interfacing- refer to page 38 for suggestions. Be sure to purchase 1/4yard of Sheer-weight Pellon Sew-in interfacing for buttonholes.
4. Buttons, Thread, and 1 1/2 yards Rayon Tape or Seams Great.

*Pretreat Fabric & Interfacing*

Follow our instructions . Refer to the chapter on preparing your fabric, page 46 .

*Before You Sew*

1. Read the entire blouse chapter.
2. Read your pattern's instructions.
3. Note differences on your pattern and refer to the book where they appear.
*Most of our students find the book's instructions the only ones they need.*

## Cut

Refer to cutting chapter (page 52 ),
and take your time.

*Special Cutting Tips*

*For a softer look we have rounded the collar
and cuffs. This makes the garment easier to pipe,
too. Round the collar and cuff points using a
glass as your guide to create a smooth even curve.

* Your collar will roll and lie better if the undercollar
is cut on the bias. Cut the top collar on grain and
then place the bottom collar on the bias. *Mark your
undercollar with a contrasting thread if you are
worried about confusing the two.*

* If your pattern has a one-piece cuff, cut it along
the fold line and add 5/8" to that side. Use that as
your pattern. (Instead of cutting 2 cuffs, you will
now need to cut 4.)

* Cut front facing 1/2"
longer at top.

* Cut interfacing on
straight-of-the-grain.

## Mark

Because of the simple design lines, most marking
can be done with snip-marks and dressmaker's
pencil dots. Refer to page 58 if necessary.

Mark the wrong sides of all pieces if you have any
doubt about which side is the right side.

# Bodice

1. Stitch fronts to back,
at shoulders and sides,
using french seams (page 72).

2. Press seams toward back.

## Neck & Collar

*Prepare Neck Edge for Collar*

To insure a strong neck edge we combine
staystitching with a reinforcing stitch.

1. Start 3/8" before large dot on front.
(This dot indicates collar placement).
Reinforce stitch (15-18 per inch) through
large dot & 3/8" past it, just inside the
seam line.

2. Change stitch length to 10-12 per inch
and staystitch along edge until you are almost
at the shoulder seam.

3. Reinforce-stitch through shoulder area,
and staystitch along back. Repeat this
stitching process until you are 3/8" past
large front dot.

*DON'T SKIP THIS STEP! You may need to
clip the neck edge when applying the collar.
This row of stitching will keep the fabric from
being unduly stressed.*

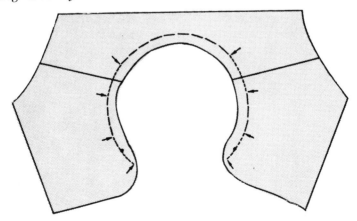

*Prepare the Collar*

1. Trim 1/8" off the unnotched edge of the undercollar. This will keep the bottom part from showing after the collar is attached.

2. Reinforce-stitch through dots.

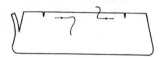

3. Apply interfacing to wrong side of top collar, using 1/2" seam allowance. Trim interfacing close to stitching. Reinforce-stitch over dots.

4. Clip to dots, and press  1/2" fabric to wrong side between dots.

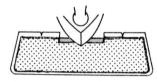

5. Stitch the top and under collar together along unnotched edge, right sides facing. Trim and press the seam open as much as possible. *Remember: the undercollar is slightly smaller than the top collar.*

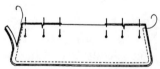

6. Turn collar to right side and press, matching the notched edges. Baste these edges together, leaving the space between the dots unstitched.

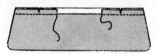

## Apply Collar

1. Pin collar to neck edge, clipping edge where necessary. Stitch, but don't trim yet.

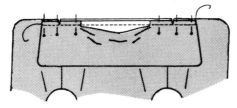

2. Place blouse on a hanger while you prepare front facing.

## Front Facing

### Prepare Front Facing

Give your facing a finished look-face-your-facing!

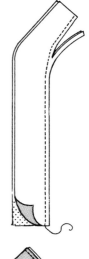

1. Place the right sides of the facing and interfacing together. Stitch along unnotched side only, using a 1/4-3/8" seam allowance.

2. Trim seam allowance and press. Press seam open.

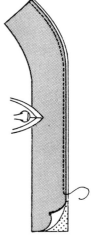

3. Fold wrong sides together and press. Baste raw edges together. Press. A great look!

## Apply Front Facing

Remember the extra 1/2" we had you add to the top of the facing? That was because the facing has a slight bias cut to the top, causing it to "shrink" sometimes, or at least readjust itself, before you apply it. Adding the extra amount is just a way to prevent possible frustration, allowing the facing to be attached easily and fall correctly.

1. Pin the facing to the garment, turning under the raw edges of facing ends. Stitch.

2. Trim and turn facings to inside. Press gently. *Pressing the seam open helps it turn more easily.*

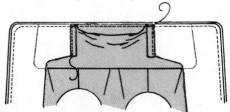

## Finish Collar and Facing

1. Pin your facing and collar in place, just over the seam line.

2. You can hand-stitch the collar and facing top in place....or *Stitch-in-the-Ditch!* Fast & Easy.
a. Turn the garment to the outside, and machine stitch in the "well" of the seam (right over the stitches themselves).
b. Stitch between the shoulder seams to catch the collar, and then in the shoulder seams for about 2" to catch top of facing.

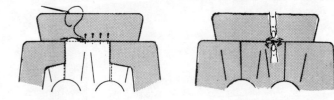

*Hang blouse on a good hanger while you prepare sleeves.*

# Sleeves

*Apply Sleeve Plackets*

1. Cut two bias strips of fabric 1 1/2" wide and 8-9" long.

2. Reinforce stitch along sleeve placket line, making one small stitch across point. Slash to point.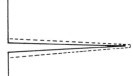

3. Right sides together, match the edge of bias strip to the edge of sleeve placket line. You do not need to pin.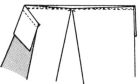

4. Place fabric under presser foot, wrong side of sleeve facing up. Start stitching, using small stitches, 1/4" from edge. As you stitch keep the bias strip 1/4" from needle. *No, the sleeve placket line won't stitch at an equal distance throughout. Yes, your placket will be even because you are keeping the bias strip at 1/4" the whole time.*

5. Cut off any extra length on bias strip. Press strip away from sleeve on right side.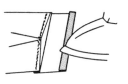

6. Turn to wrong side and press under 1/4" along bias strip. Press this over seam line and stitch in place, by hand or machine.

7. Stitch a short diagonal line at top of binding on the wrong side; this helps keep it in place. Turn in one side of binding (the side that will be on top; the buttonhole side) and baste in place.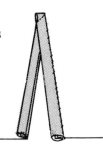

## Sleeve Seam & Gathers

1. French seam your sleeve edges together. Press toward <u>front</u>.This eliminates excess bulk later.

2. Gather the bottom edge of sleeve. See page <u>62</u> for instructions.

## Prepare Cuffs

1. Decide which cuff will be the under cuff and trim 1/8" off unnotched edge of it.Press a little less than 5/8" along notched edge, and set aside.

2. Stitch interfacing to top cuff, just inside seam line. Trim interfacing to stitching.

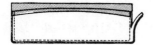

3. Stitch top and bottom cuffs together, right sides facing. Remember: the bottom cuff will be slightly small. Trim seam, press open and turn to right side. Press.

## Apply Cuffs to Sleeves

1. Stitch cuffs to sleeves, right sides together. Gather evenly.

2. Finish by hand or machine as you did the collar.

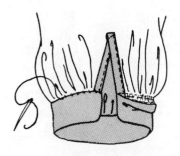

*Apply Sleeve to Bodice*

1. Stitch one or two rows of easing in sleeve cap. (See easing, page **62** ).

2. Right sides facing, pin sleeve in place, matching notches and dots. As the sleeve is eased into place make certain that the top of the cap is *not* eased. It is on the straight-of -the-grain and should remain so. Keep ease-free space 1" on either side of sleeve cap.

3. Stitch. To smooth out small puckers press the sleeve from the inside, using plently of steam. Remove the easing stitches if that will allow the sleeve cap to press more smoothly.

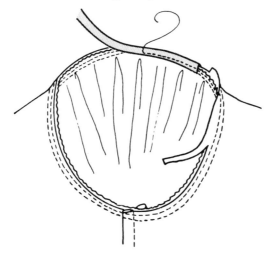

4. Stitch again 1/4" away from first stitching. Trim close to second row. You can leave this as is for your finish, or give it a custom touch. *Custom touch:* Apply rayon tape, pressed in half, over the raw edges. Or use Seams Great.


*Note*
You may wish to trim only between lower notches on tailored blouses or dresses. The remaining seam allowance will act as a small sleeve head for a smooth look. The method above is best for lightweight fabrics in soft garments.

## Hem

1. Fold the front facing *out* and stitch a small hem along bottom edge. (See page 82 )

2. Turn facing to inside and tack. If facing doesn't rest comfortably, readjust it up or down until it hangs correctly.

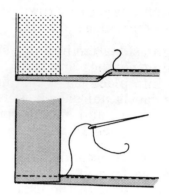

## Buttonholes Buttons

See their chapters on pages 79-81 .

## Finishing

Give your blouse a final light pressing and allow it to hang overnight. Then...wear it, wear it wear it! You have just made a thoroughly custom constructed garment that will last for years and bring you much praise. And, just think; a dress only takes another yard to make. What are you waiting for?!

## Quick Outline

1. *Make purchases*
2. *Prepare fabric & interfacing*
3. *Cut & mark fabric*
4. *Join front to back*
5. *Prepare neck edge for collar*
6. *Prepare collar*
7. *Apply collar*
8. *Prepare front facing*
9. *Apply facing & finish collar and facing*
10. *Apply sleeve plackets*
11. *Seam sleeve*
12. *Prepare & apply cuffs*
13. *Apply sleeve*
14. *Hem*
15. *Apply buttons and buttonholes*
16. *Finish*

# EXTRAS

## Piping

Piping adds a classic touch to almost any garment. Selected and sewn properly, this trim is a *gourmet sewing feat!*

The biggest mistake we have seen in piped garments is the use of the wrong kind--using a polyester/cotton piping in a silk crepe de chine, for example. No matter how well it is applied, the piping won't lay correctly.

Silk piping is a rare find. Acetate and Rayon pipings are availabe in many colors and are suitable for a wide range of silk and synthetic fabrics.

Choose piping as you would a shaping material. Place the piping next to a folded piece of your fabric and move the two together in a waving motion. Do they move well? No buckling? The cord isn't too small or large for the silk? Fine. Buy it.

Can't find what you want?

Don't waste hours shopping for a perfect match or size when the piping is at your fingertips--use your fashion fabric.

1.   See Cutting Bias Strips on page 57 , making strips about 2" wide.

2.   Buy small cording, cotton string, polyester/cotton cable cord, pearl cotton thread or strands of buttonhole twist to use as your filler. If you select 100% cotton, be sure to preshrink it.

3.   With the right side out, fold your fabric over the cord lengthwise.

4.   Stitch next to cord using your zipperfoot. Press, butting your iron up against the cord. If the cord feels a little loose, stitch again.

## How to Apply Piping

Follow these steps for easy and perfect results.

1. Baste along the fabric edge, 1/2" from edge. Press to smooth out any ripples. This will be your seam guide.

2. On the right side of your fabric pin the piping in place, with the corded edge falling just over the basted line. (In place of pins you can lightly tape the piping in place, lengthwise or crosswise. Remove the tape after stitching.) When you have done one or more applications you won't need this step.

3. Using the zipper foot, stitch next to the cord, butting the foot right up to the cord. This will automatically nudge the piping onto the normal 5/8" seam line. Good.

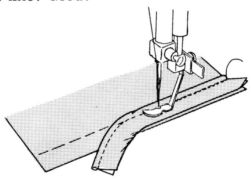

4. Turn fabric to wrong side and press. This smooths out the fabric and eases the thread in place.

5. Pin & stitch fabric pieces together, right sides facing, using a 5/8" seam. Your previous stitching line will act as a guide.

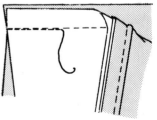

6. TURN YOUR FABRIC OVER AND RESTITCH LINE. This helps insure that the piping is sewn right up to that cord on both sides. DON'T SKIP THIS STEP! Press.

7. Trim and/or grade seams. Turn and press lightly. You may wish to edge-stitch next to the piping.

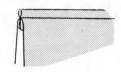

*Extra Application Tips for Piping*

\*Clip or notch where necessary when applying it to a curve or square.

\* When stitching piping around something, like a neckline or hem:
1. Cut piping 2" longer, and remove the cording from 1" of each end. (Just remove a few machine stitches and pull out 1" of cord using a pair of tweezers. Clip off the 1".)

2. Curve each end into the seam allowance, as shown, overlapping the ending piece.

or

1. Remove 1" of cording from piping. Leave this end for finishing piece.

2. Start stitching 1/2" from end of piping that still contains cord.

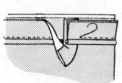

3. Stop stitching about 2" from end of row, or joining point. Fold under the raw edge of piping end (the one with the filler removed), and wrap this around the 1/2" of loose piping that started the row. Stitch over both, enclosing all raw edges and creating a smooth even look.

## French Piping

On sheer fabrics, we use french piping in place of normal pattern facing pieces. You can use this on any lightweight material.

1. In place of facings, cut bias strips 1-3/4 - 2-1/2" wide, the length of the area to be covered. See Bias Strips, page 57 for cutting instructions.

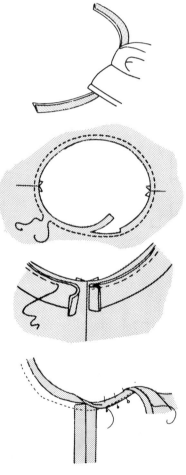

2. Fold strip in half lengthwise, wrong sides in and press in a slight curve.

3. Staystitch edge to be finished--neckline, armhole, etc. Trim 1/4" from seam line.

4. Right sides together, pin and stitch piping to garment edge, using a 1/4" seam. Trim to 1/8".

5. Turn piping to inside, just to seam line, or slightly over it. Machine or hand stitch piping in place. Half of the french piping will remain on the right side.

6. Ends can be folded in and stitched.

You can add a decorative touch to your garment by making the french piping out of contrasting material. It will create a piped look which is how this finish got its name!

# Tucks

Jan loves tucks, and enjoys using silk broadcloth and crepe de chine, and polyester georgette to best highlight them. To make beautiful tucks easily, try this method:

1. Snip the top & bottom tuck lines. (Snip top only if tuck is not full-length.)

2. Pin or use a modified tack to mark bottom of short tucks, or center dots of long ones.

3. Wrong sides together, fold tuck in half lengthwise and press. You will now have a straight edge to use as a seam guide. (You may want to place a few pins along the edge of slippery fabrics.)

4. Measure the width of the tuck, using your pattern piece as the guide. Most tucks measure 1/8-5/8" wide when folded.

5. Stitch along the width of tuck, keeping fabric taut. Presto! Albert Nipon couldn't have done better.

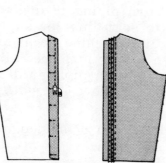

*Note*
We press and then stitch all tucks at one time. Your stitching will be more consistent. And, unless the fabric is super slinky, we rarely need to pin the tucks. Pressing creates a perfect seam guide for us. Try it!

# Casings

When making a dress with an elastic waistline your pattern will usually call for you to use a polyester/cotton bias tape for the casing. This doesn't sit well with us- literally. This type of tape can appear bulky when applied to lightweight fabrics. Also, the elastic won't slip through easily, so the garment must be constantly adjusted.

*Make a Ribbon Casing*

Using an Offray satin ribbon will create a casing that is smooth, flat and rests comfortably against your slip or skin.

1. Select a ribbon that is 1/4" wider than your elastic, and 2" longer than the casing line.

2. Apply to your garment as the pattern directs, stitching close to the ribbon edges, turning in 1" on each end.

For a sheer fabric:
1. Pick a ribbon that is close to your fabric in color. Buy two widths; one ribbon should be 1/2" wider, and the other 1/4" wider than your elastic.

2. Apply the widest ribbon first, folding the ends toward you.

3. Apply the second ribbon over the first, stitching close to the edges, turning the ends toward the other ribbon. Insert the elastic between the two ribbons.

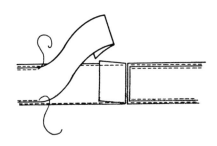

# Bias Comments

The use of fabric cut on the bias was first made popular by Madeleine Vionnet in the early part of the century. She revolutionized the fashion world with her superbly designed and draped clothing.

No wonder. Bias cut clothing is flattering to any figure, falling smoothly over the body, then swirling out at the hem. The cut is also a comfortable one to wear. Give yourself at least one bias cut garment.

*Tips for Cutting and Sewing on the Bias*

* Cut carefully, using lots of pins. The fabric will seem to grow as you cut if not pinned securely.

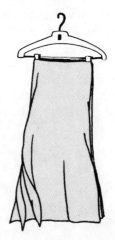

* Once cut, hang the pieces for 24 hours to allow the fabric to adjust to its new position. DON'T skip this step or your garment will hang unevenly.

* Use 14-16 stitches per inch, and treat the fabric like a knit, stretching slightly as you sew.

* Use a thread with give: silk or polyester, not cotton.

* When joining a bias piece to a straight cut piece keep the bias on top so you won't stretch the straight piece, An example: joining skirt to waistband. Keep waistband underneath.

* Don't overfit. Because bias cut fabric has so much ease you may be tempted to take-in and take-in. Be reasonable in fitting or you will cause ugly wrinkles across the fabric.

* Zippers can pose a slight problem if not applied with care. A wavery pooch occurs when you attach a stable type zipper to an unstable bias seam. Work with the fabric, using a lightweight coil zipper sewn in by hand (see page __76__ ).

* Tape any area, like shoulder seams, that you want to stablize. See page __63__ for instructions.

* Don't hem until you allow the final garment to hang for two or three days. You will have "just another failure" if you skip this step.

* Measure hem from the floor to assure a perfectly even bottom edge.

* If you avoid bias cut clothes because they fall a little too close to the body, underline or line the garment. Cut these on the bias, too. You'll love the results.

Note

Many custom houses regularly cut linings on the bias. It creates a more comfortable inner garment, and an expensive one. Why not just cut a blazer sleeve lining on the bias? It will slip on easily and feel more comfortable when you move your arms.

Note

Any supporting piece should be cut on the straight of the grain: waistbands, straps,etc.

# Lingerie

Silk slip? Isn't that a bit extravagant, you ask?
Not when you consider the following:

* We've seen synthetic slips selling for $30, $40
even $50! A silk slip wouldn't cost a penny more.

* A silk slip is more than just a comfortable
undergarment. You can wear it as a camisole
blouse, tucked into skirts, as an underdress for
sheer garments or as an after-five sheath to
wear with evening wraps. Four garments in one!

* Silk slips can be made in such pretty colors.

* A slip is fast and easy to make!

## Basic Silk Slip Suggestions

* Look for a slip pattern that will be cut on the bias;
it will fit and drape better.

* Look for patterns using small yardage; camisoles
require about 1 1/4 yards & slips about 2.

* If you are a C-cup or larger buy your pattern one
size larger; bias garments don't allow as much ease
at the bustline, the most important area to fit with
this garment.

*Charmeuse, satin and crepe de chine make the best
silk slips.

* Cut your straps on the straight-of-the-grain; they
are the slips main support, and bias cut straps can
stretch out of shape easily. For added support fold
the strap over ribbon.

* Making a camisole top? Cut it longer than the pattern
requires so you can tuck it into slacks and skirts,
or blouse it as a top.

* Your initial investment in this little treasure will repay
you for years; Jan's Grandma had silk slips that were
40 years old!

# SPECIAL TOPPINGS

## Elegance in Under 1 Hour

There is something about a silk evening garment that makes the night seem magical. But, sewing one can be scary business to a newcomer to silk. We offer you two fashions that fit and flatter any figure type, and are easy to make as well. In fact, one woman saw them displayed at a fashion show we presented and decided she would make both- even though she had never sewn a stitch in her life! A few days later she called to say her *creations* received so many raves she was going to learn how to sew everything!


*THESE SENSUOUS BEAUTIES-*

* *Have no zippers, buttonholes or facings.*

* *Require no purchased patterns.*

* *Can be made in less than 1 hour.*

* *Fold flat for storing or travelling.*

* *Are Sew Wonderful!*

# Cheryl's Sheath

This is Cheryl's version of "the little black dress."
The dress was *draped into being* the same day she
was to attend a fashion event.

1. Purchase: 2 1/4 yards silk or synthetic, 45" wide.
      4 1/2" buttons
      Silk buttonhole twist, or 1/2 yard small cord.
      Thread

2. Have on Hand: Scraps of Sheer-weight pellon or woven
interfacing, and a belt or sash.

3. Pretreat fabric.

4. Hem all edges 1/2"
by hand or machine.

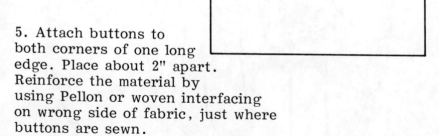

5. Attach buttons to
both corners of one long
edge. Place about 2" apart.
Reinforce the material by
using Pellon or woven interfacing
on wrong side of fabric, just where
buttons are sewn.

6. Place a pin in top center of
long edge. Make four thread loops
(or attach cord) long enough to
fit over buttons. Position two of
these 7" from pin mark and two
5" from mark.

*Thread Loops*

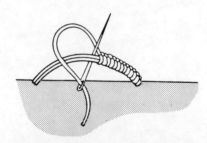

7. Wrap as shown.
Put belt or sash on and
adjust drape until hem
is even and straight.

The dress will measure
40-43" long. A wider fabric
will give you a longer length.
Extra yardage will give you
more fullness and drape.

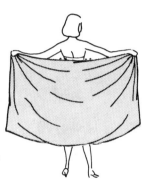

Cheryl has received many compliments on her dress,
made from black silk charmeuse. That first evening
she was asked several times about her new *Halston,
Calvin Klein or "Is that from the recent Bill Blass
Collection?"* designer dress. "No," she replied,
demurely, "it's just a little something I threw
together."

*NOTE*
*Be sure to secure this dress with a belt. Because of
its ultra drapey quality an underdress (or camisole)
should be worn.  A silk slip is perfect!*

# Jan's Ravishing Wrap

Jan saw this in a high-fashion magazine, at a high-fashion price, modified it and made it a versatile garment that can be worn several ways.

1. Purchase: 2 3/4 yards of any drapey fabric, 40-45" wide. Thread.

2. Pretreat fabric.

3. Cut 4" off one selvage. (Cut 1/2" off if fabric is 40" wide.) Hem all raw edges 1/4". (You can speed this along by using your hemmer foot, page 83 ).

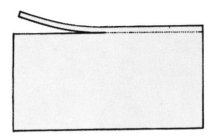

4. Right sides together, pin short sides together and sew a 1/4" seam 18" long. Start at the top of the selvage edge (the only edge you did not have to hem.) Press seam open.

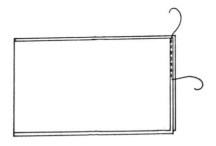

5. Bring this seam to the center of the selvage edge. Pin right sides together and stitch a 1/4" seam across the entire edge.

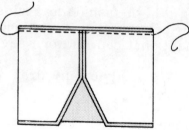

6. Make armholes by measuring 11" down from top of long seam, and cutting a 1" scoop from the folded sides. Start at the top edge, 1" in, and end by curving out at pin mark 11" down. It looks like a curve.

7. Hem the armholes with a small hand or machine roll.

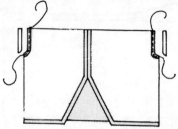

8. Wear as shown, over dresses, pants, anything! Make a tie from the excess fabric you cut in Step 3.

*Note*

If you are very tall buy 3 yards. Short, 2 1/2 yards.

# Little Treats

*Small items you can make with silk*

Save those scraps! You can make wonderful little gifts with silk remnants- pincushions, sachets, contrasting collars and cuffs to attach to completed garments, and so much more. Anything made with silk is something special.

We have developed a nifty buying trick to allow us to splurge-with-the-urge to give silk gifts to our friends and family without going broke. When we see a wonderful silk or synthetic that reminds us of someone nice, we buy 1/4-1/2 yard of it. There are two things we can always make with that small amount:

1. A long fringed scarf. Even at $60 per yard, that ultra exquisite satin-striped-chiffon-with-a-screened-print can be made into a gorgeous accessory for $15.
   a. Buy 1/4 yard of 45" wide silk.
   b. Hem long edges, and stitch across two ends just where you to fringe.
   c. Pull out one thread across the short rows. Great activity when watching TV.

2. Hankerchieves. More women are wearing these in blazer pockets, or tied around their necks. 1/3 yard will make 3 hankerchieves. Even at $36 per yard, each hankerchief will only cost $4!
   a. Buy 1/3 yard of silk. Cut three squares 12"X12" each. Hem all sides.

# Care

Give quality care to quality clothes and your clothing will maintain their value through years of wear.

Two major enemies of any fabric are:
1. Perspiration.
2. Wrinkles.

## PERSPIRATION

Perspiration and deodorant wreak havoc on fabrics, literally rotting them. Since most of us perspire and use some form of deodorant, what can be done?

Using dress shields in any blouse or dress will prevent unnecessary damage to fine fabrics. They come in various shapes and sizes, and are easy to apply. You can tack them in, pin them, or, as our friend Kristi does, snap them in place!

Shields are sold mainly in department stores, but more fabric stores are carrying them, too. Ask! If no one in your area sells these, or if you don't like the ones ready-made, make your own.
a. Trace the bottom of your armhole, between the notches.
b. Cut 2-4 layers of cotton flannel, muslin or cotton blend.
c. Finish all raw edges and stitch into garment.

## WRINKLES

When a garment is tossed carelessly over a chair and wrinkles develop, you tend to treat the garment with less respect. "Oh, that dress? I was planning on having it cleaned anyway, so why hang it up?"

Your clothes will stay clean and wear longer if they are always placed on a hanger to air out and relax after wearing. Silk repels soil and hanging will give it a chance to release excess dust. Do this even if the garment is to be cleaned before you wear it again.

## LAUNDERING SILK....A FEW NOTES

Most washable silks will be laundered the same way you pretreated them on page 49 . There are a few extra notes we would like to add.

* A few of the high-sericin silks (raw, noil, pongee) can sometimes be machine washed, using a mild soap and a delicate cycle. You can test a scrap, ask the store and/or check the fabric label.

* If you do wash any silk in the machine, keep in mind that agitation can irritate dyes and fibers. Place the garment in a nylon mesh bag to lessen possible damage. Hang to dry, and press while the garment is slightly damp.

* Keep white silks white by adding 3 tablespoons of white vinegar to the final rinse water.

* Hard water can make fluid silks feel a little crisp. Add a mild hair conditioner to your rinse water, just as you would to your hair.

* Do not dry silks in the sun. Even your hair responds poorly to continued exposure to this element.

# DRYCLEANERS....THEY ARE NOT MAGICIANS

Drycleaning is a <u>wet</u> process. The cleaning solvents are wet solutions <u>that</u> don't contain water. Garments are washed in this liquid and then placed in a *reclaimer* that removes the cleaning agent. Then it is pressed.

Pressing involves three units:

1. A *Suzy* is an air-bag form that blows up to provide a torso shape for your garment. It releases air, steam and/or heat from the inside out.

2. The *Header* looks like two ironing boards that form a sandwich to steam and press. The top is usually known as *the header*.

3. A hand iron. Just a plain old iron.

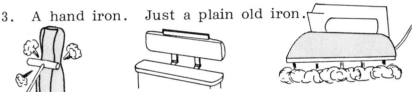

No magical gadgets will be found at your drycleaners. So what are you paying for when you take your clothing to be cleaned? Good question. When your silk cannot be hand washed, a coin-operated cleaning place may be ideal for you--and a money-saver. BUT, a good drycleaner can work miracles on a silk garment that has been stained. Professional stain removers can do what you can't--use chemical blends, in just the right mixture, to save a damaged fabric.

*A good drycleaner* always asks you if there are any special problems, stains, pressing, etc., when you take clothing in.

*A good customer* remembers where, when, and what the problems are: sleeve, last night, chocolate fondue.

*We save time and money by having drycleanables cleaned <u>only</u> and not pressed. Fine silks require less pressing so we do the touch-ups ourselves, saving almost <u>half</u> in cost.*

# Where to Wear Silk

*ANYWHERE!*

*Except to a tax audit....you're going to look like a*

*MILLION!*

# BRIEF INDEX

If additional copies are not
available in your fabric store,
you may order directly:

Send $5.95 + 1.00 postage and handling to:

SEW WONDERFUL, INC.
P.O. Box 31928
Seattle, WA 98103

Send check or money order only.
PLEASE do not send cash. Thank You!

# A GOURMET SEWING FEAST!

Sew Wonderful
Gourmet Garments

a guide to fashion-without-frustration,
with 10 simple & sensational designs

by Cheryl Arrants

$6.95

The "menu" includes:

* Timeless Fashions, feminine & flattering
  for sizes 6-22
* 10 Patterns for less than 70¢ each
* Minimum ingredients- a dress from 1½ yards
* Dresses, blouses, pants, skirts, even a <u>coat!</u>
* Spiced with unique  buying & sewing tips.

<u>By Cheryl Arrants</u>, author of Sew Wonderful Silk.

If this book is not available in your fabric store,
please send $6.95 + 1.00 postage to:
Sew Wonderful, PO Box 31928, Seattle, WA 98103